D1453041

A HANDBOOK FOR CHURCHWARDENS AND PAROCHIAL CHURCH COUNCILLORS

In memory of

Colin Fawcett, QC

for many years Churchwarden of
St James' Church, Gerrards Cross,
to whom I owe so much.

T.J.B.

A Handbook for
Churchwardens
and
Parochial
Church Councillors

The late

Kenneth M. Macmorran QC, MA, LL.B

Formerly Chancellor of the Dioceses of Chichester, Lincoln, Ely, St Albans, Newcastle and Guildford

and

Timothy J. Briden MA, LL.B

Of the Inner Temple, Barrister-at-Law; Vicar-General of the Province of Canterbury; Chancellor of the Dioceses of Bath and Wells, and Truro

continuum
LONDON • NEW YORK

Continuum
The Tower Building, 11 York Road   15 East 26th Street
London SE1 7NX   New York, NY 10010

First published in November 1921
New editions 1957, 1966, 1971
Thirty-seventh impression, revised, 1973
Thirty-eighth impression 1975
New editions 1977, 1978, 1980
Reprinted with amendments 1982
Reprinted with further amendments 1983
New editions 1986, 1989
Reprinted 1990, 1991, 1992, 1993, 1994
New edition 1996
Reprinted with amendments 1997
Reprinted 1998
New edition 2001
Reprinted 2004
New edition 2006

British Library Cataloguing-in-Publication Data
A catalogue record for this book is available from the British Library.

ISBN 0-8264-8152-3 (hb)
     0-8264-8153-1 (pb)

Designed and typeset by Kenneth Burnley, Wirral, Cheshire
Printed and bound in England by Antony Rowe Ltd, Chippenham

Contents

Introduction

Chancellor Kenneth Mead Macmorran (1883–1973) wrote extensively on the subject of ecclesiastical law, although this is the only book which still bears his name. Changes in the law, reflected in successive editions published since his death, have resulted in the loss of much of the text as written by him. The repeal of the Churchwardens (Appointment and Resignation) Measure 1964 has brought about another step in this process. Nevertheless, Chancellor Macmorran's fundamental purposes in creating the original Churchwardens' Handbook remain unchanged. The first of these is to provide a simple guide to the legal functions of churchwardens and parochial church councillors. The second is to include, in a single, convenient volume, the actual legislation which may have to be consulted on a day-to-day basis within parishes. Although the legislative appetite of the General Synod has caused the quantity of enacted material to grow to substantial proportions, there is really no substitute for the text of a Measure or Rule when addressing the practical questions which so often arise. Hence the original scheme of reproducing the relevant legislation, with editorial notes, has been retained. In this edition, however, attempts are being made to ease the reader's task by providing some diagrams to illustrate the more common legal procedures. A table of contents for that lawyer's paradise known as the Church Representation Rules has also been included.

The principal changes to the current edition have, however, been brought about by the passing into law of the Churchwardens Measure 2001 and the Clergy Discipline Measure 2003. The opportunity has also been taken to provide an expanded chapter concerning the legal powers and duties of parochial church councils, who find themselves increasingly beset by the demands of secular legislation.

I am grateful for the interest taken in this book by correspondents. My particular thanks are due to the Reverend Lisa Battye for pointing out various infelicities in the text.

Timothy Briden

1 The Constitution of the Church

THE PROVINCE

The Province of Canterbury, consisting of 30,[1] and the Province of York, consisting of fourteen, dioceses, together constitute the Church of England as far as this country is concerned. This work is not concerned with the other Churches in communion with the See of Canterbury and the overseas provinces. Each of the Provinces of Canterbury and York is under the direction of an archbishop, and both the archbishops preside over dioceses as well as exercising their archi-episcopal authority in their respective provinces.

An archbishop is president of his convocation and he issues his mandate for the assembly of that body on receipt of a writ from the Crown. During a vacancy in the see of a diocese within the province he provides for the ecclesiastical administration of that diocese in his capacity of 'guardian of the spiritualities'[2] for the whole province. He normally nominates a suffragan or assistant bishop for the purpose. It is his duty to consecrate new bishops, including suffragan bishops, although his participation in the consecration is not necessary to its validity. A bishop holding

---

1   The thirtieth being the diocese in Europe, incorporated into England (for ecclesiastical purposes) in 1980. For obvious reasons, its constitution cannot wholly accord with that of the other dioceses, and this book omits further reference to it. Sodor and Man and that part of the diocese of Winchester which comprises the Channel Islands also provide special cases with which this book does not deal.

2   A vacant arch-see is administered by the dean and the chapter. In the case of several of the more ancient dioceses, when there is a vacancy in the see, it is customary for the archbishop to delegate the guardianship to the dean and chapter of the cathedral church of the diocese. The Dean and Chapter of Durham claim to be the guardians of spiritualities of that diocese during a vacancy. The claim is not admitted by the Archbishop, but in fact it is the Dean and Chapter who act.

office within the province swears an oath of canonical obedience to the archbishop.

The Archbishops of Canterbury and York have the special styles respectively of Primate of All England and Metropolitan, and Primate of England and Metropolitan. Both of them are always members of the House of Lords.

THE DIOCESE

The diocese is a defined territory presided over by a bishop, who has an exclusive jurisdiction within it. In some statutes and in the Book of Common Prayer, the bishop is spoken of as the 'ordinary', i.e. as having ordinary jurisdiction in ecclesiastical matters within his diocese. This denotes an original as distinct from a delegated jurisdiction exercised by the diocesan bishop.

The principle which underlies the whole system of the spiritual government of the Church is that of vesting the government of each diocese in the bishop of that diocese. This dominant idea is to be seen in actual working every day. Thus no bishop may presume to exercise any episcopal function in the diocese of another without the consent of the diocesan, and he may be inhibited from so doing. Again, the diocesan bishop institutes an incumbent to the cure of a parish, and that incumbent has no rights therein until the institution has taken place. Nor has an assistant curate any right to officiate until he or she has been licensed by the bishop. Nor can a lay person assume the office of reader without the bishop's permission.

At the same time, the Anglican episcopate is a constitutional episcopate and not an absolutely monarchical one. In this respect the bishop is bound in several ways. He is the centre and head of his diocese, and the unity of the Church requires that this should be so. But at his consecration he takes an oath of obedience to the archbishop, and he is bound to govern his diocese in accordance with the law of the Church.

It is, perhaps, hardly necessary to add that in ruling his diocese, a bishop must conform to the secular law so far as it is applicable. His duties are regulated in innumerable matters by common law and statute, and so far as these are of intimate concern to the laity, mention is made of them in their appropriate context in the chapters which follow.

In addition to the two archbishops, the Bishops of London,

Durham and Winchester, together with 21 other diocesan bishops according to seniority of appointment as diocesans, have seats in the House of Lords.

In most, though not all, dioceses, the diocesan bishop has the assistance of one or more suffragan bishops. Every suffragan bishop, on his appointment, is accorded a titular see, which is invariably, in practice, named after some place within the diocese.

A suffragan bishop is, in law, appointed for the diocese as a whole, and not to any particular area within the diocese. But under the Dioceses Measure 1978, s. 10, a diocesan bishop has power to make a temporary delegation to a suffragan bishop of any of his functions within a specified area. And s. 11 of the Measure contains provisions under which a reorganization or other scheme, made according to the procedure laid down by the Measure, may provide for the division of a diocese into areas (called 'episcopal areas') and for specifying the bishop (being either the diocesan or a suffragan bishop) or bishops (being the diocesan bishop and a suffragan bishop) who are to have or share the episcopal oversight of each area. But the making of any such scheme is not to be taken as divesting the diocesan bishop of any of his functions (which will accordingly continue to be exercisable by him at his discretion throughout the diocese).[1]

Dioceses are divided into archdeaconries, which in turn consist of rural deaneries. These units are interposed between the parish and the diocese for certain purposes, although the two latter are the only units necessary to a parochial system. It follows that as a general rule each parish is in (1) a rural deanery, (2) an archdeaconry, (3) a diocese, and (4) a province. The two latter have been briefly described.

THE ARCHDEACONRY

An archdeaconry may extend to the whole of a diocese, but is usually smaller. At its head is the archdeacon, who on appointment must have completed at least six years in priest's orders. The Archdeacon is usually (though not always) appointed by the bishop,

---

1   Thus the Diocese of London has, in accordance with these provisions, been divided by scheme into five episcopal areas.

and before entering upon office subscribes the declaration of assent set out in Canon C15,[1] and takes the oath of allegiance. An archdeacon is entitled by custom to the style of address 'The Venerable'.

Subject to the paramount rights of the bishop of the diocese, an archdeacon has the power of visitation within the archdeaconry, and it is at the archdeacon's visitation after the end of April (when the bishop does not hold one) that churchwardens are admitted to office.

The Care of Churches and Ecclesiastical Jurisdiction Measure 1991 gives to the archdeacon important responsibilities including the granting of faculties in certain cases. In addition, powers are conferred on the archdeacon for the enforcement of the provisions for the quinquennial inspection of churches contained in the Inspection of Churches Measure 1955. The archdeacon also 'inducts' clergy who are presented to benefices, i.e. places them in possession of the *temporalities* of the benefice.

The archdeacon is a member of the Diocesan Board of Patronage when the board is transacting any business relating to a benefice in that archdeaconry.

THE RURAL DEANERY

The rural deanery is a collection of parishes for administrative purposes within an archdeaconry. Its significance as an ecclesiastical unit has been enhanced as a result of the creation, by the Synodical Government Measure 1969, of deanery synods, in which important functions are vested.[2]

Each rural deanery is presided over by a rural dean who is usually (though not necessarily[3]) one of the beneficed clergy in the deanery. The rural dean is the bishop's officer and may be removed from office at any time.

Apart from this and a few other statutory functions, the rural dean's duties are such (e.g. of inquiry and report about specific matters) as may from time to time be delegated by the bishop or archdeacon. According to some authorities the rural dean may, in the absence of the archdeacon, 'induct' to a benefice: but it is doubtful whether this may be done except with the permission of the archdeacon.

---

1   As to the nature of this declaration, see p. 30 footnote 1.
2   See p. 7.
3   It is lawful for a deacon to be appointed to the office of rural dean.

The rural dean, and an elected member of the house of laity of the deanery synod, jointly chair that synod. In that capacity the rural dean is also a member of the Diocesan Board of Patronage when the Board is transacting any business relating to a benefice within the deanery.

SYNODICAL GOVERNMENT

Historical background

Before 1919, the Sovereign in Parliament was the only institution having unlimited power to legislate for the affairs of the Church of England. An Act of Parliament could (as it still can) effect any alteration whatever in the law of the Church.

A subsidiary legislative power was vested in the two Convocations of Canterbury and York, bodies composed entirely of bishops and clergy which, after a long lapse, had been revived in 1852 and 1861 respectively. Each Convocation had power to legislate by passing canons, but it was a strictly conditional and limited power. In the first place a canon, to be effective at all, required the royal assent; secondly, it was only effective within the province whose Convocation passed it; thirdly, it was ineffective in so far as it conflicted with existing common law or statute; and finally, a canon was directly binding only on the clergy and holders of ecclesiastical offices (such as churchwardens) but not on the laity generally.

The Church of England Assembly (Powers) Act 1919 gave legal authority to the body called 'The National Assembly of the Church of England' ('The Church Assembly' for short) in which was vested a general power, subject to the control of Parliament, to legislate upon matters concerning the Church of England.

Stated very briefly, the general scheme of the Act was as follows. The Church Assembly, as constituted by the Act, consisted of three Houses: the House of Bishops, the House of Clergy (both derived from the Convocations), and the House of Laity. Power was conferred on the Assembly to propose and pass new laws called 'Measures'. Any measure, having been passed in the Assembly and having been (in effect) endorsed by resolution of both Houses of Parliament, and having received the royal assent, was given the same force and effect as an Act of Parliament.

The Synodical Government Measure 1969, whilst building on the scheme of Church government established in 1919 and subsequent years, introduced such considerable alterations and reforms that it created a more or less entirely new system. Under the scheme introduced by the Measure, 'synods', each of them with a mixed clerical and lay membership, were established at the national, diocesan and ruri-decanal levels; such synods being known as the 'General Synod', 'diocesan synods' and 'deanery synods' respectively.

The General Synod

The General Synod, though continuous in identity with the former Church Assembly, was largely re-constituted, and it inherited not only the power of the Church Assembly to legislate by measure, but also the former power of the Convocations to make canons (which power was transferred to it from the Convocations). It is also empowered to pass subordinate legislation, and to make regulations (known as 'Acts of Synod') in cases where a measure or canon would be inappropriate. Apart from its legislative powers, the General Synod conducts debates upon matters of religious or public interest.

Diocesan synods

A diocesan synod is composed of three houses: a house of bishops, a house of clergy and a house of laity. Its functions are to consider matters concerning the Church of England and to make provision for such matters in relation to the diocese; to consider and express an opinion on other matters of religious or public interest; to advise the bishop on any matters on which he may consult the synod; and to consider and express an opinion on any matters referred to it by the General Synod.

It is the duty of the bishop to consult with the diocesan synod on matters of general concern and importance to the diocese.

The diocesan synod is enjoined to keep the deanery synods of the diocese informed of the policies and problems of the diocese and of the business which is to come before meetings of the diocesan synod, and it may delegate executive functions to deanery synods. It is also enjoined to keep itself informed, through the deanery synods, of events and opinions in the parishes, and to give opportunities at its meetings for discussing matters raised by deanery synods and parochial church councils.

Deanery synods

A deanery synod consists of a house of clergy and a house of laity. It exercises at deanery level deliberative powers similar to those of the diocesan synod, as well as bringing together the views of the parishes in the deanery on common problems, making known provisions made by the diocesan synod, considering the business of the diocesan synod, and raising such matters with it as the deanery synod considers appropriate.

Deanery synods are enjoined to exercise any functions which may be delegated to them by the diocesan synod in relation to the parishes of their deaneries, and in particular (if so delegated) the determination of parochial shares in 'quotas' allocated to the deaneries (meaning the amount to be subscribed to the expenditure authorized by the diocesan synod).

2 The Courts of the Church

DIOCESAN COURTS

The law relating to ecclesiastical courts and the trial of ecclesiastical cases was much revised, and to a large extent codified, by the Ecclesiastical Jurisdiction Measure 1963, as amended by the Care of Churches and Ecclesiastical Jurisdiction Measure 1991.

Under these Measures (as previously), every archbishop (in his diocesan capacity) and every diocesan bishop has a court for the trial of ecclesiastical matters arising in his diocese. In the Diocese of Canterbury this court is known as the commissary court and elsewhere as the consistory court. The judge of the court is, in Canterbury, styled the Commissary General and in other dioceses the Chancellor. In this book, the expressions 'consistory court' and 'chancellor' are intended to cover the diocesan court and its judge in every diocese including Canterbury.

The chancellor is appointed by the bishop. The candidate must be at least 30 years old and a barrister or solicitor of seven years' standing, or a person who has held high judicial office; and if the bishop appoints a lay person, he must satisfy himself that the appointee is a communicant. It is no longer necessary to secure the chancellor's tenure of office through confirmation by the dean and chapter (or the cathedral chapter) of the cathedral church.

The chancellor remains in office until death or resignation, subject (in the case of a chancellor appointed on or after 1st March 1965) to a power for the bishop to remove a chancellor resolved by the Upper House of the Convocation of the province to be incapable of acting or unfit to act; and subject also (in the case of a chancellor appointed on or after 25th April 1976) to compulsory retirement by reason of age.

The status of the bishop in his own court depends upon the terms of the patent appointing the chancellor. In some cases the bishop expressly reserves to himself the power to sit and try certain cases or classes of cases. But except so far as this power is reserved, the chancellor is the sole judge, and indeed may try cases to which the bishop himself is a party.

The consistory court remains the court of first instance only for the trial of faculty cases (see Chapter 3). Formerly it was also responsible for the trial of proceedings against priests or deacons for offences not involving any matter of doctrine, ritual or ceremonial. The Clergy Discipline Measure 2003 has, however, transferred the hearing of complaints about these matters to new disciplinary tribunals specially established for the purpose.

PROVINCIAL COURTS

The provincial courts of Canterbury and York are known respectively as the Court of Arches (or Arches Court of Canterbury) and the Chancery Court of York.

The principal judge of both courts is appointed by the two archbishops subject to the approval of the Queen; in the Province of Canterbury the judge is styled 'Dean of the Arches', and in that of York 'Auditor'. Of the other judges in each court, two are clergy appointed by the prolocutor of the Lower House of Convocation of the relevant province; two are communicant lay persons possessing judicial experience, appointed by the Chairman of the House of Laity of the General Synod after consultation with the Lord Chancellor; and the remainder are all of the diocesan chancellors except the chancellor of the diocese in Europe.

Each provincial court is the court of appeal from the consistory courts within the province in faculty cases not involving matters of doctrine, ritual or ceremonial (for the hearing of which cases the Dean of the Arches or Auditor sits with two diocesan chancellors); also in proceedings against priests and deacons for offences not involving such matters (for the hearing of which all five judges other than the chancellors sit).

In faculty cases there is a further appeal from the provincial court to the Judicial Committee of the Privy Council.

COURT OF ECCLESIASTICAL CAUSES RESERVED

This court consists of five judges appointed by the Queen. Two of them are persons who hold or have held high judicial office and who are communicants, and the other three are persons who are, or have been, diocesan bishops. All decisions are by a majority of the judges.

This court is the court of first instance for proceedings against the clergy for offences against the laws ecclesiastical involving matters of doctrine, ritual or ceremonial. It is also the court of appeal from consistory courts in faculty cases involving such matters. In either class of case, there is a final appeal from the Court of Ecclesiastical Causes Reserved to a Commission of Review, consisting of three lay Lords of Appeal who are communicants, and two diocesan bishops who are members of the House of Lords.

PROCEEDINGS FOR MISCONDUCT

A new system for dealing with complaints against the clergy for misconduct has been created by the Clergy Discipline Measure 2003. For this purpose misconduct covers both acts and omissions involving breaches of ecclesiastical law; neglect or inefficiency; and unbecoming or inappropriate conduct. Matters involving doctrine, ritual or ceremonial fall outside the scope of this Measure, and continue to be subject to the Ecclesiastical Jurisdiction Measure 1963.

Within the Clergy Discipline Measure 2003 procedures concerning archbishops and bishops are kept separate from those which apply to priests and deacons. Since cases involving the episcopate are specialized in nature, this section will concentrate upon the position of priests and deacons in proceedings for misconduct. A simple diagram, showing the procedure in outline, is on page 11.

The starting point is a written complaint from a person having a proper interest in making it. This includes the victim of alleged misconduct as well as a churchwarden of a relevant parish or a person nominated by resolution of the parochial church council.[1]

The complaint is referred to the diocesan registrar, whose task is to consider whether the complainant has a proper interest, and whether the complaint is of sufficient substance to justify further action. The purpose is to filter out complaints which are procedurally defective or lack merit.

---

1 The resolution must be passed by a majority of two-thirds of the lay members present at a meeting attended by at least two-thirds of the lay membership as a whole.

Proceedings for misconduct

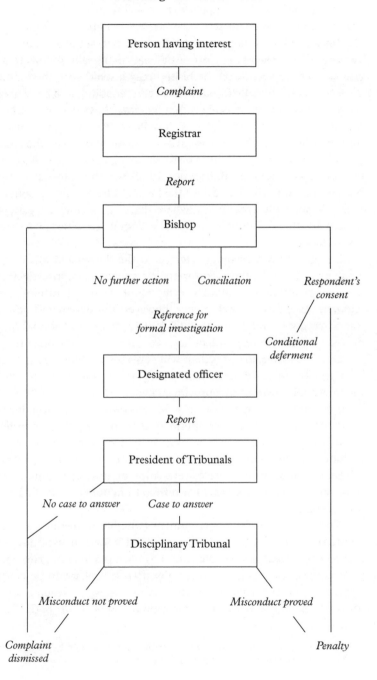

The registrar next reports to the bishop, who has to decide whether to dismiss the complaint or allow it to proceed. If the complaint is not to be dismissed, there are several choices available to the bishop. One is simply to take no further action.[1] With the consent of the respondent priest or deacon (usually following an admission of misconduct) the bishop may instead keep the matter on record conditionally for up to five years, enabling it to be revived if a further complaint is made within the time allowed, or the bishop may impose one of the penalties set out below. Another possibility is for the bishop to cause an attempt at conciliation between the complainant and the respondent to be made, using the services of a conciliator agreed between the parties. In all the above instances the matter does not proceed beyond the bishop. The remaining course, which is normally appropriate where there are serious allegations denied by the respondent, is for the bishop to direct a formal investigation.

The matter is thereupon referred to the designated officer, in effect an independent prosecutor made responsible for investigating the complaint and ultimately bringing it before a disciplinary tribunal. As a further preliminary, however, the designated officer has to prepare a report so that the president of the tribunal may decide whether the respondent has a case to answer. Provided there is a case to answer, the president will convene a tribunal consisting of a legally qualified chairman with two lay and two ordained members, all drawn from a provincial panel.

It is for the tribunal to hear evidence on oath and adjudicate upon the complaint. If the respondent is found to have committed the misconduct in question, a range of penalties may be imposed including prohibition from exercising ministry for life or for a term of years; removal from office or revocation of licence; an injunction requiring the respondent to do or refrain from doing a specified act; and a rebuke.

Where a sentence of imprisonment (whether immediate or suspended) has been imposed by a criminal court, or a finding of adultery or unreasonable behaviour has been made in matrimonial proceedings, there is no need for a written complaint to be made against the person concerned. Instead the priest or deacon automatically becomes liable to prohibition, removal, or both. The

---

1   There is an appeal to the president of tribunals against a bishop's decision to dismiss a complaint or to take no further action upon it.

bishop imposes the penalty after consulting the president of tribunals and considering any representations made by the respondent.

Rights of appeal to the Court of Arches and the Chancery Court of York have been preserved by the Measure.

PROCEEDINGS CONCERNING DOCTRINE, RITUAL OR CEREMONIAL

If the complaint against a priest or deacon involves a matter of doctrine, ritual or ceremonial, the bishop, after giving both the accused and the complainant an opportunity of being interviewed in private, must decide either that no further step is to be taken, or to refer the complaint to a specially constituted committee for inquiry. Such committee consists of one member of the Upper House and two members of the Lower House of the Convocation of the province, and two chancellors of dioceses in the province. No further steps are to be taken in the matter if the committee, after due inquiry, decides that there is no case for the accused to answer, or alternatively that, although there is a case for him to answer, the offence is too trivial to warrant further proceedings, or that there were extenuating circumstances, or that further proceedings would not be in the interests of the Church. If, however, the committee recommends further proceedings, the Upper House of Convocation has to nominate a fit person to promote a complaint against the accused in the Court of Ecclesiastical Causes Reserved, and the case is brought before that court accordingly. There is provision whereby the court, in the trial of any case, will have the assistance of three to five expert advisers. If the court finds the accused guilty, it decides on and pronounces the appropriate censure; but no censure more severe than monition can be pronounced in the case of a first offence.

3 Faculties

The consecrated buildings and lands situated within a diocese are in the ultimate guardianship of the bishop, who exercises his authority in this respect through his chancellor. In consequence the legal proceeding known as the application for and the granting of a faculty is necessary for the sanction of alterations in a consecrated building or its contents, or in a churchyard or other consecrated burial ground or its contents.

The faculty jurisdiction extends to unconsecrated land which forms, or is part of, the curtilage of a consecrated church (Faculty Jurisdiction Measure 1964, s. 7). It may also be extended, by an order of the bishop, and during the period specified in such order, to any unconsecrated building which he has licensed for public worship before 1st March 1993 (s. 6).

The petition for a faculty is lodged in the consistory court of the diocese. An unconsecrated building licensed after that date for public worship is subject to the faculty jurisdiction unless the bishop otherwise directs. The petition is usually made in the name of the incumbent and churchwardens, but this is not necessary since any person who is regarded by the law as having an interest is entitled either to apply for or to oppose the grant of a faculty; and for this purpose all the following persons are regarded as having an interest: the parishioners, persons who though not resident in the parish are on its electoral roll, and the archdeacon;[1] and also in some types of case, certain other persons as well.

The object of obtaining a faculty is to ensure that the work proposed to be done shall not subsequently be interfered with, for if anything is done without the grant of a faculty, it is open to any parishioner, or other person having an interest, to apply for a faculty

---

1 See Care of Churches and Ecclesiastical Jurisdiction Measure 1991, s. 16. If the archdeaconry is vacant, or if the archdeacon is incapacitated or unable or unwilling to act, the bishop may appoint another person to act.

authorizing the removal of the work. In such a case the incumbent and churchwardens, or any other person or persons also having an interest, may lodge a cross-petition for a confirmatory faculty authorizing retrospectively what is sought to be removed.

Trivial additions to the church or its furniture, e.g. almsboxes or hassocks, do not require a faculty.

As regards the churchyard, no faculty is necessary for the burial of a body; on the other hand, a body cannot be removed from consecrated ground for burial elsewhere without a faculty. For the erection of a monument, a faculty is required in strict law, but usually this is not insisted on in practice, and the incumbent's approval is regarded as sufficient. If approval is refused, the person desirous of erecting the monument can petition for a faculty to reverse his decision.[1]

Trivial repairs or replacements do not require a faculty. The chancellor of each diocese is required to give written guidance concerning minor works which may be undertaken without a faculty. The guidance usually takes the form of a list of insignificant repairs or alterations. Where minor works outside the scope of the list are contemplated, it is prudent to ask the chancellor whether a faculty is needed.

No faculty may be granted for anything illegal, e.g. because it has a superstitious purpose, or because it would be inconsistent with the sacred purposes for which the building or land is consecrated. But within the limits of legality, the consistory court has an extremely wide discretion to give or refuse a faculty for almost any sort of work or innovation. This discretion must, however, be exercised judicially and for proper reasons. Certain conditions and restrictions are imposed by the Care of Churches and Ecclesiastical Jurisdiction Measure 1991 on the grant of a faculty for the demolition or partial demolition of a church. The jurisdiction of the consistory court is generally limited to those places where the bishop is the ordinary.[2] He is the ordinary for most of the geographical area

---

1 In many dioceses the chancellor has issued a Directive indicating the nature of the monuments (size and type of stone) which are usually considered suitable for that locality and has indicated that, within the terms of the Directive, he is content for the incumbent to permit their introduction without the need for a faculty. The legal effect of such a Directive is open to doubt; but in practice such schemes work well, and, since the jurisdiction of the consistory court cannot be ousted, it is open to any interested party to have recourse to the court.

2 See p. 2. Certain chapels and other places of worship were also brought within the jurisdiction by the Care of Places of Worship Measure 1999.

covered by the diocese, but not for places known as peculiars, for example, Westminster Abbey, nor usually (and perhaps surprisingly) for his cathedral church where in most cases the dean is the ordinary and sometimes the dean and chapter fulfil that role. This book is not concerned with such, usually non-parochial, places.

There is in every diocese an Advisory Committee whose function it is to assist the chancellor on the one hand and the parishioners on the other. These committees usually consist of experts in architecture, archaeology, and art, who know the diocese and its churches. Before they lodge a petition intending applicants are required to seek the guidance of the Advisory Committee. It is essential to provide the Committee with detailed plans and specifications. A site visit is sometimes appropriate. After considering the proposals the Advisory Committee will issue a certificate indicating whether or not they are recommended, alternatively the certificate may simply state that no objection is raised. The receipt of an unfavourable certificate does not preclude the presentation of a petition for a faculty, but in considering the case the chancellor is entitled to take account of the advice given by the Advisory Committee. The advisory committee system has justified itself by results, and considerable attention is given by chancellors to the views of the committees. A Council for the Care of Churches also exists, the purpose of which is to co-ordinate the work of the diocesan committees and to advise in cases which present special difficulty.

The responsibility for adjudicating upon faculty petitions has, since the enactment of the Care of Churches and Ecclesiastical Jurisdiction Measure 1991, been divided between chancellor and archdeacons. The power to issue an archdeacon's certificate has been abolished; instead, where the petition is unopposed, if the Advisory Committee recommends the proposals and the work is of a nature specified in Appendix A to the Faculty Jurisdiction Rules 2000, the jurisdiction to grant a faculty is exercised by the archdeacon. All other petitions are placed before the chancellor.

In a simple case, where there is no opposition, a chancellor may, and commonly does, grant a faculty without a hearing in court. Furthermore the chancellor now has power, with the consent of the parties, to reach a decision after considering written representations alone, thus avoiding the expense of the court hearing. Where, however, at least one party desires an oral hearing, or the chancellor (irrespective of the parties' wishes) considers that an oral hearing is appropriate, the consistory court is convened, often in the parish in which the dispute has arisen.

There is a special procedure to cater for the temporary reordering of the interior of a church. No faculty is needed; instead, on the application of the minister and the majority of the parochial church council the archdeacon may issue a written licence permitting the scheme for a period not exceeding twelve months. The archdeacon has, however, no jurisdiction to grant a further licence covering the same scheme after the twelve-month period has expired. Instead, the interior must be restored to its previous condition or the new arrangements must be authorized by faculty.

If the church is a listed building, English Heritage, one or more of the National Amenity Societies[1] and the local planning authority have the right to make representations about proposed changes to the fabric or important fittings. In such cases, it is appropriate for the parochial church council to prepare a Statement of Significance (which identifies the important features of the church) and a Statement of Need explaining the reasons for the intended change. The Statements should be used when informing interested parties of the proposals. Early consultation with the Advisory Committee, English Heritage and the appropriate amenity society is highly desirable, as it is likely to result in a measure of agreement and thereby to save time and expense. Even if agreement in principle is secured at the outset, the consultees will probably wish to see the detailed designs and plans before giving their final approval. In the absence of prior agreement to the proposals, the chancellor will have to direct special notice to the interested bodies after the petition has been lodged, so that they may, if they wish, oppose the granting of a faculty.

OBTAINING A FACULTY

This diagram illustrates the method of obtaining a faculty in a straightforward, unopposed case. Where the proposals are not recommended by the Advisory Committee, or the petition is opposed, advice about procedure should be sought from the Diocesan Registry.

---

1   The National Amenity Societies are as follows (dates of specialization shown in brackets): Society for the Protection of Ancient Buildings (before 1715); Georgian Group (1700–1840); Victorian Society (1837–1914); Twentieth Century Society (1914 onwards).

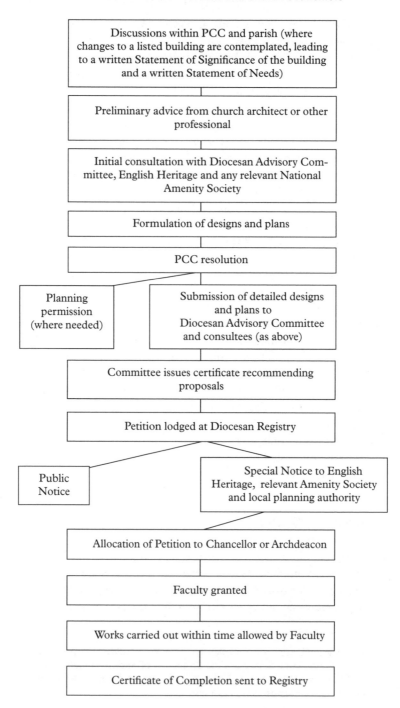

Discussions within PCC and parish (where changes to a listed building are contemplated, leading to a written Statement of Significance of the building and a written Statement of Needs)

Preliminary advice from church architect or other professional

Initial consultation with Diocesan Advisory Committee, English Heritage and any relevant National Amenity Society

Formulation of designs and plans

PCC resolution

Planning permission (where needed)

Submission of detailed designs and plans to Diocesan Advisory Committee and consultees (as above)

Committee issues certificate recommending proposals

Petition lodged at Diocesan Registry

Public Notice

Special Notice to English Heritage, relevant Amenity Society and local planning authority

Allocation of Petition to Chancellor or Archdeacon

Faculty granted

Works carried out within time allowed by Faculty

Certificate of Completion sent to Registry

4 The Parish

ANCIENT PARISHES

A parish is an area committed to the incumbent by the bishop for the cure (i.e. care) of souls. Within the parish the incumbent is, under the bishop, supreme, but this supremacy is constitutional and not arbitrary. The incumbent is the bishop's deputy for most purposes within the parish, exercising 'the cure of souls' to the exclusion of other clergy.[1]

The growth of the parochial system was a gradual process. While the bishop is the incumbent, and the cathedral is the parish church, of the whole diocese, and the only essential 'parson' for the existence of a diocese is the bishop with his cathedral church, it became necessary at an early stage for him to have assistants in his ministrations. It may be mentioned that the term 'parson' is really a corrupt abbreviation of *ecclesiae persona* or 'ecclesiastical person'. The first stage of parochial development was for the bishop to ordain clergy to assist him in the diocese, who were then sent out by him to preach and administer the sacraments in any district to which he might assign them. As yet no churches existed, and the clergy resided with the bishop where his *cathedra* or 'seat' was. In course of time, churches were built and endowed, and they required clergy to

---

1   This exclusive right of the incumbent is modified by the Extra-Parochial Ministry Measure 1967, which entitles a minister of any parish to perform offices and services at the home of a person who is on the electoral roll of that parish but resident in another parish, without the consent and free from the control of the minister of that other parish; and which also empowers the bishop of a diocese to license a clergyman to officiate within the diocese in the premises of any university, college, school, hospital, or public or charitable institution, without the consent and free from the control of the minister of the parish in which the premises are situated. A further exception, regarding funeral services in crematoria or cemeteries, is made by section 2 of the Church of England (Miscellaneous Provisions) Measure 1992.

minister in them. The person who built the church usually nominated a layman for ordination to the cure, or a priest to perform the duties there. Very often the founder of the church was the local lord of the manor. In this growth of church buildings we see the beginnings of the right to present clergy to incumbencies, a right vested in some person, not necessarily the bishop, which is familiar at the present day. The person in whom the right is vested is now known as the 'patron', whose status is historically derived from the 'lord' responsible for building a church on his demesne, and nominating the man of his choice as the minister of that church. The country gradually became covered with churches, each of which served a district which coincided more or less with a political area, and these districts are the predecessors of the parishes of modern times. While this was the normal process, it sometimes happened that the bishop would assign a district to a church, and place one of his clergy there. But, however the local conditions varied, the priest who served each church was called 'curate', as a person to whom the cure of souls was delegated. The districts assigned to churches came to be called parishes; and by the end of the thirteenth century practically the whole realm had been divided up into parishes, and the ecclesiastical units so formed are now termed '*ancient* parishes'.

NEW AND ALTERED PARISHES

As was to be expected, changed circumstances, especially increases in the population of urban and suburban areas, demanded modifications in the scheme of ancient parishes. From the early nineteenth century onwards, a number of Acts of Parliament, notably the Church Building Acts 1818 to 1884 and the New Parishes Acts 1843 to 1884, were passed to enable new parishes or districts to be created where they were required. For all practical purposes, all these Acts were repealed and replaced by the New Parishes Measure 1943, the relevant provisions of which have now themselves been repealed, and replaced successively by the Pastoral Measure 1968 and the Pastoral Measure 1983.

Numerous parishes have been created over the years under these various statutes and are now in existence. Although they are in fact modern ecclesiastical units, the law relating to them is, for practical purposes, virtually the same as the law relating to ancient parishes.

Statutory provisions

The only statutory provisions now in force for the creation of new parishes, or the alteration of existing ones, are those contained in the Pastoral Measure 1983 itself. This Measure provides for the establishment in every diocese of a Pastoral Committee, and for the making by the Church Commissioners of 'pastoral schemes', based on proposals submitted by the Pastoral Committee with the approval of the bishop; any such scheme takes effect on its being confirmed by Order in Council. At various stages in the proceedings leading to the making and confirmation of a scheme, there are provisions for ascertaining the views of 'interested parties' (who include, amongst others, all incumbents, patrons and parochial church councils liable to be concerned); for giving notice, both in the press and to particular persons, of the objects of the intended scheme and of its submission for confirmation; and for dealing with any written representations which may be received with respect to it. Any person who has made written representations with respect to a scheme, and whose objections have not been met, may apply for leave to appeal to the Judicial Committee of the Privy Council; and the scheme will not be confirmed until the appeal has been decided.

New benefices or parishes

Amongst the matters for which a pastoral scheme may provide are the following: the creation, by union or otherwise, of new benefices[1] or parishes; the dissolution of existing benefices or parishes; and the alteration of the areas of existing benefices or parishes (including the transfer of a parish from one benefice to another) or the definition of their boundaries.

There are wide powers in the Measure for enabling a scheme to deal with churches in the area to which it extends. If the scheme makes no provision with respect to the churches in the affected area, they simply retain their pre-existing status. Any church in the new or altered parish may, however, be designated as the parish church or as an additional parish church, and the Measure enables there to be more than one parish church or additional church within the parish. A new church provided under a scheme may become the parish

---

1   As to the meaning of 'benefice', see p. 23.

church or an additional parish church once it has been approved by the Church Commissioners and consecrated.

A scheme may create a new parish with full parochial status although there will be no parish church when the scheme comes into operation. In such a case, and in any other case of a parish having no parish church, as soon as a church within the parish is approved by the Church Commissioners and is consecrated, it becomes the parish church. Meanwhile, the bishop is enjoined to license one or more buildings or parts of buildings for public worship; he may also designate any building or part of a building so licensed as the 'parish centre of worship', whereupon, so long as the designation remains in force, it is deemed to be the parish church for all legal purposes, including the solemnization of marriages. (This does not affect the right, under the Marriage Act 1949, of parishioners intending to be married to resort for the purpose to the church of an adjoining parish until their own parish has an actual parish church. Meanwhile, they have an option in the matter.)

Redundant churches

Any church in an area affected by a scheme which is deprived by the scheme of the status of a parish church, or which does not acquire that status under the scheme, will either continue in use as a chapel-of-ease, or be declared redundant by the scheme. The Measure lays down a complicated procedure for dealing with redundant churches which it is beyond the scope of this book to describe in detail. As a rule, unless there is some suitable use to which a redundant church can be put or for which it can be disposed of by sale or otherwise, it is liable eventually to be demolished; but there are special provisions concerning the preservation of churches of historical or architectural interest.

Some of the powers conferred by the Measure may be exercised by a 'pastoral order' instead of by a pastoral scheme. The procedure for making an order is relatively simple: the order is proposed by the Church Commissioners and made by the bishop; no confirmation by Order in Council is necessary, and there is no appeal to the Judicial Committee of the Privy Council. But any proposals for the creation or dissolution or union of benefices or parishes, or for transferring any church used for public worship from any benefice or parish, or for making any church redundant, can only be given effect to by a scheme.

UNIONS OF BENEFICES AND PARISHES

Within the context of the parochial ministry, a benefice may be defined as the office of the rector or vicar (i.e. of the incumbent) of a parish. Thus a union of benefices, without more, entails simply the concentration of both or all of the incumbencies of two or more parishes, as one office or benefice, in the hands of one incumbent. The identity of the parishes themselves is not affected; each of them remains a separate parish, with its own parish church and parochial organization. The only essential legal link between them is that their combined incumbencies have become a single office, held by a single incumbent whom they share.

A union of parishes necessarily involves a union of the benefices of the parishes concerned. But it also entails the loss, by each of those parishes, of its separate identity, and the merger of both or all of them into a single new united parish.

The Pastoral Measure 1968 repealed and superseded all the earlier legislation relating to unions; and any proposed union of benefices or parishes can now only be effected by a pastoral scheme under the provisions outlined above. The Measure of 1983 contains full powers for the purpose, and in particular declares that a pastoral scheme providing for the union of two or more benefices may provide for uniting all the parishes within the area of the new benefice, or for uniting some but not all of them, or leaving them as separate parishes.

TEAM AND GROUP MINISTRIES

Since the enactment of the Pastoral Measure 1968 there have been experiments based on the idea of an association of clergy co-operating in the running of an area considerably larger than a normal parish.

In different places there may be different reasons for such an arrangement. In some areas (mostly rural) it can be an effective method of coping with a shortage of clergy, by deploying the available clergy to the best advantage. Elsewhere, in thickly populated built-up areas (such as a 'new town' or a suburb of recent growth) a considerable modification of the ordinary parochial system may be thought desirable, on account of the difficulty of dividing an area of this sort into parishes of normal size, each capable of existing as a separate community with a life of its own. Yet another possible advantage of these arrangements is the scope and opportunity they can offer to clergy with specialist training or talents.

The Pastoral Measure 1983 affords a legal basis for team and group ministries, by enacting that a pastoral scheme may provide for the establishment of a ministry of either of these two sorts. It also contains provisions defining and safeguarding the status of the clergy engaged in them.

Team ministry

A team ministry is a ministry which normally covers the area of a single benefice, although it may be extended to the area of two or more benefices if and so long as all such benefices are held in plurality by the same incumbent. Any benefice concerned may, as a result of a union of benefices, contain any number of separate parishes. Under the provisions of the Measure, the incumbent of the benefice or benefices is styled 'rector', and is the principal member of the team. The other clergy in the team are styled 'vicars'.

Group ministry

A group ministry is a ministry covering two or more benefices with different incumbents, the general principle being that each incumbent will, besides attending to his own benefice, assist the incumbents of the other benefices.

Either a team or a group ministry may be dissolved by a subsequent pastoral scheme.

Comparison

Broadly, the contrast between a team ministry and a group ministry is that the former operates on the basis of a team under a leader (the incumbent or 'rector'), whilst the latter is a partnership of equals, each of whom is an incumbent with primacy in the area of a particular benefice.

Both types of ministry are primarily concerned with the organization of clerical staff within a particular area; and the status and duties of the participating clergy will be more particularly considered in the next chapter. But in relation to both of them, the Measure also contains special provisions for such matters as patronage and parochial church councils, and these provisions will be noted, later in this book, under the appropriate heads.

CONVENTIONAL DISTRICTS

Conventional districts are sometimes formed in anticipation of their subsequently becoming distinct parishes; they are unaffected by the Pastoral Measure 1983. They are not parishes, but merely areas which are placed, with the consent of the incumbent and the bishop, under the care of a 'curate-in-charge' upon whom devolves the responsibility for the cure of souls in the district. The arrangement requires renewal with every change in the incumbency of the parish in which the district lies.

So long as a conventional district exists, it has an organization similar to that of a parish. In particular, it has its own churchwardens, electoral roll and parochial church council.

Conventional districts are now the only sort of 'ecclesiastical districts' capable of existing in law. The Pastoral Measure 1968 converted all other districts then existing into parishes, and abolished the machinery for creating new ones.

SHARING OF CHURCH BUILDINGS

The Sharing of Church Buildings Act 1969 was passed with the general object of facilitating agreements (termed 'sharing agreements') for the sharing and use of church buildings by different Christian bodies. Where a parish or other church of the Church of England is the subject matter of a sharing agreement, or where the competent authorities of the Church of England enter into a sharing agreement in relation to a church belonging to some other Christian body, or to a church proposed to be built, this is likely to have a considerable effect on the life and organization of the parish concerned.[1]

The Churches which may be parties to a sharing agreement include the Church of England, the Roman Catholic Church, and all the principal Free Church bodies. Any two or more of such Churches may enter into a sharing agreement with respect to any existing or proposed church building or buildings. In the case of the Church of England, the Diocesan Board of Finance of the diocese

---

1 Although the statements in the text are primarily concerned with the sharing of places of worship, it should be mentioned that sharing agreements can also be made under the Act with respect to church buildings of certain other types: parish halls, youth clubs or centres, and places of residence for ministers or lay workers.

concerned, and the incumbent and parochial church council of the parish concerned, are necessary parties to any sharing agreement; and the consent of the bishop and the Pastoral Committee of the diocese must also be obtained. The necessary parties to a sharing agreement on behalf of the Roman Catholic Church or any Free Church are such persons as may be determined by the appropriate authority of that Church.

Ownership

As regards ownership, a sharing agreement may provide for the shared buildings or building to be owned by one only of the sharing Churches or to be jointly owned by all or some of them. But this is subject to the qualification that any existing consecrated church of the Church of England must remain in the sole ownership of the Church of England, unless authority is given by a pastoral scheme to provide for joint ownership by the Church of England and another Church or Churches. An unconsecrated church building which is the subject matter of a sharing agreement is not permitted to be consecrated, unless under the agreement it is in the sole ownership of the Church of England. And any church building which is shared by the Church of England under a sharing agreement may only become or remain a parish church if, under the agreement, it is in the sole ownership of the Church of England; but even if it is not in such sole ownership, its designation as a 'parish centre of worship'[1] is permissible.

A sharing agreement must make provision (amongst other things) for determining the extent to which any church building to which it applies is to be available for worship in accordance with the forms and practice of the sharing Churches; and for dealing with financial obligations as to repairs, furnishings, etc. It must also contain appropriate provisions for its own termination.

GUILD CHURCHES

The status of 'guild churches' is peculiar to the City of London, and is the creation of the City of London (Guild Churches) Act 1952 (a private Act). Although guild churches are not parish churches, the

---

1   See p. 22.

Act gives them a comparable organization and it is convenient to mention them briefly here.

The status was devised as a method of dealing with the special circumstances obtaining in the City, where on the one hand there are far more churches than are necessary for the needs of resident Sunday worshippers; but on the other hand, there is on working days a vast influx of non-residents who are proper objects of pastoral care, and many of whom are attendants at weekday services in City churches.

A number of former parish churches in the City have been converted into guild churches under the Act of 1952, or the City of London (Guild Churches) Act 1960 (which amended it in certain respects). As such, they no longer have the status of parish churches; nevertheless, they are wholly independent of the parishes in which they are respectively situated. Each guild church has a minister, who is appointed by a patron, is licensed by the bishop, is free from any control by the incumbent of the parish, and is entitled to the style of 'vicar'. The minister's period of office, initially five years, may be extended from time to time for additional periods of three years each. In relation to the church and its churchyard the guild vicar has the same rights and duties as those of a parish incumbent in relation to the parish church and churchyard; but there is no obligation to provide Sunday services. An assistant curate may also be appointed.

As from 1st January 1976, under the Ecclesiastical Offices (Age Limit) Measure 1975, no priest aged 70 or over may be appointed vicar of a guild church, and any vicar of a guild church appointed on or after that date is subject to provisions for compulsory retirement at the age 70 or upwards, similar to those affecting an incumbent (see pp. 38–9).

Provision is made by the Act of 1952 for churchwardens and sidesmen of a guild church, for a guild church electoral roll, and for a guild church council, which is analogous to a parochial church council and similarly composed.

5 The Parochial Clergy

THE INCUMBENT

Rectors and vicars

The smallest normal unit of organization is, as has been already indicated, the parish, at the head of which is the incumbent, who has the cure of souls therein, and is either a 'rector' or a 'vicar'. The difference between a rector and a vicar is historical rather than practical. Briefly, it may be said that where the whole of the tithe and glebe were attached to the benefice for the maintenance of the minister, that benefice is a rectory. Where there is a mere vicarage, a monastery formerly had the rights of the rector, and took the glebe and tithe whilst providing a vicar to attend to the parochial duties. At the dissolution of the monasteries, laymen became rectors in place of the monasteries and took the tithe.

Previously to the Pastoral Measure 1968, there was a third class of benefice called a perpetual curacy, which arose where the incumbent was neither a rector, nor was an endowment provided out of the income of the rectory for his maintenance; the benefices of new ecclesiastical parishes were as a rule perpetual curacies. But the Measure converted all perpetual curacies into vicarages. The incumbencies of districts converted by the same Measure into parishes are likewise vicarages.

On a union, by a pastoral scheme, of two or more benefices one of which is a rectory, the new benefice created by the union is a rectory. And on the dissolution of a rectory under a pastoral scheme, otherwise than as a result of a union of benefices, the benefice in the area of which the residence of the rector of the dissolved benefice is situated is likewise a rectory. But except in those two cases, or in the case of a team ministry, every new benefice created by a pastoral scheme is a vicarage.

In the context of team ministries, the expressions 'rector' and 'vicar' have special meanings which are considered later in this chapter.

Institution and collation

An incumbent is 'presented' to the bishop by the patron of the benefice, except where the bishop himself is the patron. The incumbent is put in possession of the cure of souls by the bishop by a process known as institution, or, where the bishop is patron, as collation.[1]

Under the Benefices Act 1898, the bishop can refuse to institute a presentee on the ground that at the date of presentation not more than three years have elapsed since the presentee was made a deacon; or on the ground of the unfitness of the presentee by reason of physical or mental infirmity or incapacity, or serious pecuniary embarrassment, or for any of the moral reasons specified in the Act; or on the ground of the presentee's having, with reference to the presentation, been knowingly party or privy to any transaction or agreement which is invalid under the Act.

Under the Benefices Measure 1972, the bishop may also refuse to institute on the ground that the presentee (not having previously held a benefice or been a vicar in a team ministry) has had less than three years' experience as a full-time parochial minister.

If the bishop refuses to institute on any of these grounds, the patron or the presentee has a right of appeal to a special court constituted by the Act of 1898.

By virtue of the Ecclesiastical Offices (Age Limit) Measure 1975, no priest aged 70 or over may be presented or collated to a benefice.[2]

Before the incumbent is instituted, the notice of the bishop's intention to admit must be sent to the secretary of the parochial church council at least three weeks in advance and affixed to the

---

1 As to the considerable alterations in the law relating to patronage, and to rights of presentation or collation, which are contained in the Patronage (Benefices) Measure 1986, see Chapter 6, particularly pp. 51 to 62.

2 An exception is made by the Church of England (Miscellaneous Provisions) Measure 1978, s. 2, by virtue of which the Measure of 1975 is not to be taken as invalidating any provision in a pastoral scheme or order for designating a person over the age of 70 as the holder of an office, if immediately before the scheme or order came into operation, and also on 1st January 1976, he was the incumbent of a benefice affected by the scheme or order.

church door, where it must remain for two weeks, and the presentee must make the declaration of assent,[1] and take the oaths of allegiance[2] and of canonical obedience. These preliminaries are also necessary before collation.

Induction

The incumbent is put into possession of the temporalities of the benefice by the process known as 'induction', which is performed by the archdeacon on the mandate of the bishop. Induction is sometimes performed by the rural dean, but in law only as the archdeacon's mandated deputy. In practice, institution and induction take place usually at a service held at the parish church, but this is not necessary and an institution can be made even at a place outside the diocese. But induction should always be after institution, and should not precede it.

The incumbent, once put in possession of the benefice, has within it, subject only to the rights of the bishop and his officers, the exclusive duty of ministering and the exclusive rights to the emoluments appertaining to the cure.

Conduct of services

The incumbent[3] is responsible for the performance of divine service in the parish. Canon B11 requires Morning and Evening Prayer to be said or sung in parish churches on all Sundays and other principal Feast Days as well as on Ash Wednesday and Good Friday. On all other days provision is to be made for Morning and Evening Prayer either in the parish church or (following consultation with the

---

1 The modern form of the declaration of assent is set out in Canon C15 (amended as authorized by the Church of England (Worship and Doctrine) Measure 1974). Briefly, it affirms the declarant's belief in and loyalty to the faith revealed in Scripture and set forth in the Creeds, to which the historic formularies of the Church of England (the Articles of Religion, the Book of Common Prayer and the Ordinal) bear witness; and it includes an undertaking to use only the forms of service authorized by canon.

    Until recently, a declaration against simony was also required by law, but this requirement has now been abolished.

2 In certain cases of clergy who are not citizens of the United Kingdom and Colonies, the bishop has power to dispense with the oath of allegiance.

3 This responsibility is placed similarly on any other minister having the cure of souls.

parochial church council) elsewhere in the parish. Under Canon B14, Holy Communion must be celebrated on all Sundays, the principal Feast Days, Ash Wednesday and Maundy Thursday. Obvious difficulties arise in complying with these Canons where there are several churches or other places of worship in a benefice. Canon B14A therefore empowers the minister, jointly with the parochial church council, to dispense with the canonical routine on an occasional basis. Regular changes in the arrangements require the dispensation of the bishop. There has always to be a good reason for using these dispensing powers. In no case, moreover, may the changes result in a church ceasing altogether to be used for public worship.

There is also a general duty to administer the sacraments and other rites (including baptisms, marriages and funerals) as occasion requires. Except for reasonable cause approved by the bishop, a sermon must be preached at least once each Sunday (see Canon C24).

The incumbent, in addition to the services prescribed by law, may hold services at other times or in other places. Without the bishop's permission, however, the incumbent may not, in strict law, celebrate the Holy Communion otherwise than in a church or chapel, save when visiting the sick of the parish, including those outside the parish who are on the electoral roll.

As to forms of services, the position is now regulated by the Church of England (Worship and Doctrine) Measure 1974, and canons made thereunder.

Under the Measure, the General Synod is authorized to make provision by canon with respect to worship in the Church, including provision for empowering the Synod to approve, amend, continue or discontinue forms of service; and also has power to make provision by canon, or by regulation made thereunder, for any matter, except the publication of banns, to which any of the rubrics of the Book of Common Prayer relate. For the purposes of the Measure, the word 'rubrics' is defined to include all directions and instructions contained in the Prayer Book, and all tables, prefaces, rules, calendars and other contents thereof.

These general powers are, however, subject to the following limitations and conditions imposed by the Measure:

1. They must be exercised in such a way as to ensure that the forms of service contained in the Book of Common Prayer will continue to be available for use.

2. Any canon or regulation made under the powers in question, and any approval, amendment, continuance or discontinuance of a form of service, must be finally approved by the General Synod with a two-thirds majority in each House.

3. Any canon or regulation so made, and any form of service so approved (whether in its original or an amended form) must be such as in the opinion of the General Synod is neither contrary to, nor indicative of any departure from, the doctrine of the Church of England in any essential matter; but the final approval by the Synod of the canon or regulation or form of service (with the requisite majority in each House) will be conclusive that this requirement is satisfied.

4. The Measure requires it to be laid down by canon that in the case of approved services other than occasional offices, the decision as to which form of service is to be used in any church in a parish is to be taken jointly by the incumbent and the parochial church council; and further, that if they disagree, the forms to be used shall be those contained in the Book of Common Prayer unless other approved forms of service have been in regular use in the church during at least two of the four years immediately preceding the disagreement, and the parochial church council resolves that those other forms of service shall be used either to the exclusion of, or in addition to, the forms contained in the Prayer Book.

5. The Measure also requires it to be laid down by canon that, in the case of occasional offices (other than Confirmation), the decision as to which form of service is to be used will be made by the minister who is to conduct the service, but that if any of the persons concerned objects beforehand to the use of the service selected by the minister, and agreement cannot be reached, the matter is to be referred to the bishop for decision.

These provisions of the Measure have been implemented by Canons B2 and B3.

Approved Forms of Service

Canon B2 enables the General Synod (by the requisite majority in each House) to approve forms of service either with or without time limit, and to amend, discontinue, or extend the time limit on any such form of service, but so that any form of service (as approved or amended) shall be such as in the opinion of the Synod is neither contrary to, nor indicative of any departure from, the doctrine of the Church of England in any essential matter. There is now power, under Canon B5A, for the archbishops to authorize, for an experimental period, a form of service eventually intended to be approved by the General Synod.

Canon B3 lays down, in accordance with the requirements of the Measure, the manner of deciding which forms of service are to be used in any church in a parish.

Common Worship 2000 was authorized by the General Synod under the Measure.

Discretionary Arrangements

Canons B4 and B5, made in exercise of a power expressly conferred by the Measure, contain provision for services on special occasions. Under Canon B4, the Convocations of Canterbury and York (within their respective provinces), or failing any authorization by them, the archbishops within their provinces or the bishops within their dioceses may authorize special forms of service for use on occasions for which no provision is made by the Book of Common Prayer or by the General Synod under Canon B2; and under Canon B5, on occasions for which no provision is made either in the Prayer Book, or under Canon B2, or by Convocation or the archbishops or the diocesan bishop under Canon B4, the minister may use any suitable form of service.

Canon B5 also empowers a minister to make variations not of substantial importance in any authorized form of service (whether Prayer Book or otherwise) according to particular circumstances.

Versions of the Bible

As regards forms of service contained in the Prayer Book, the Prayer Book (Versions of the Bible) Measure 1965 provides that where any portion of Scripture (that is, a portion from the Authorized Version) is appointed by the Prayer Book to be read, said or sung, the corresponding portion of Scripture contained in any version of the Bible for the time being authorized for the purpose by the General Synod may be used at the discretion of the minister, provided (in the case of a church in a parish) that the parochial church council agrees, and also provided (in the case of any occasional office) that none of the persons concerned objects beforehand to its use. The versions at present authorized for this purpose are the Revised and the Revised Standard Versions, the New English Bible, the Jerusalem Bible and the Good News Bible; and also in the case of the Psalms the Revised Psalter and the Liturgical Psalter.

Dress

The dress of a minister at divine service is laid down by Canon B8. At Morning and Evening Prayer, and for the occasional offices, a surplice or alb with a scarf or stole are normally to be worn. At the Holy Communion the presiding minister is enjoined to wear similar vesture; but when a stole is worn other customary vestments may be added. It is assumed that a cassock will be worn beneath the surplice although no mention of the cassock is made in the Canon. The practice of a graduate to wear, with the scarf, the hood of his or her degree is also undoubtedly lawful even though Canon B8 is silent on the point.

The minister is not to change the form of vesture in use without first ascertaining, by consultation with the parochial church council, that such change will be acceptable; in the case of disagreement the bishop's directions must be sought and obeyed.

Incumbent's other duties

Other duties of the incumbent, as specified in Canon C24, include the instruction of children; the preparation and presentation to the bishop of confirmation candidates; visiting, particularly of the sick and infirm; and providing parishioners with spiritual counsel and advice.

The incumbent is under a duty to reside in the parsonage house if there is one, but the bishop's licence to live in another fit house, within or outside the parish, may be given. The minister must reside in the parish, unless so licensed, for nine months out of the twelve.

It is the duty of the incumbent to convene the annual parochial church meeting, and if present to act as chairman. The incumbent is also chairman of the parochial church council and, as such, responsible for convening its meetings. The responsibility for the allocation of any money collected in church falls upon the incumbent acting jointly with the parochial church council.[1]

---

1 See pp. 84 and 170.

Enforcement of duties

Formal complaints which can be made under the Clergy Discipline Measure 2003 against an incumbent (or against any other priest or deacon holding a position involving duties) for break of ecclesiastical law, or neglect or inefficiency, are considered in Chapter 2.

There are also certain special provisions under other statutes for the enforcement of particular duties. In particular, under the Pluralities Act 1838, if, not having the necessary licence from the bishop, an incumbent fails to reside in the parish for the required period in each year, a proportionate part of the annual value of the benefice is forfeit, and if non-residence persists against the bishop's order, the profits of the benefice may be sequestrated by the bishop. Further, if such a sequestration remains in force during the incumbent's absence without leave for a whole year, the benefice automatically becomes vacant.

The Incumbents (Vacation of Benefices) Measures 1977 deals with cases where there has been a serious breakdown in pastoral relationships within a parish, or where an incumbent is unable, by reason of age or infirmity, to discharge his or her duties adequately.

In cases of serious breakdown, the effect of the Measure, as amended by the Incumbents (Vacation of Benefices) (Amendment) Measure 1993, can be summarized as follows:

1. The procedure for which the Measure provides will be set in motion by a written request to the bishop for an inquiry into the pastoral position in a parish, on the ground that there has been a serious breakdown of the pastoral relationships between the incumbent and the parishioners, to which the conduct of the incumbent or of the parishioners or of both has contributed over a substantial period.

2. Such a request may be made either by the incumbent or by the archdeacon, or by a majority of at least two-thirds of the lay members of the parochial church council (in which last-mentioned case the complainants must specify two of their number to act as their representatives, and must indicate which of those two will act as 'the designated representative', i.e. will handle the correspondence relating to the inquiry).

3. Unless the request was made by the archdeacon personally, the bishop will direct the archdeacon to prepare a report and within

six weeks after receiving this direction the archdeacon must report to the bishop whether in his opinion an inquiry should be instituted.

4. If either (a) the original request for an inquiry was made by the archdeacon, or (b) the archdeacon reports that an inquiry should be instituted, or (c) the archdeacon, though not originally so reporting, informs the bishop within six months after reporting that he or she considers that the circumstances are such that an inquiry is nevertheless required, the bishop may, in his discretion, direct an inquiry. If the archdeacon reports against an inquiry, but within six months after so reporting the secretary of the parochial church council or the 'designated representative' informs the bishop that an inquiry is nevertheless required, the bishop may direct an inquiry but is not obliged to do so. The bishop's refusal to direct an inquiry may, on review, be reversed by the archbishop.

5. Any inquiry will be conducted by a provincial tribunal. A provincial tribunal consists of (a) the chairman, who must be either the chancellor of some other diocese within the same province, or a Queen's Counsel who is a communicant member of the Church of England; (b) two clerks in holy orders from a panel appointed from the members of the Lower House of Convocation; and (c) two lay persons from a panel appointed from the members of the House of Laity of the General Synod. The inquiry is a judicial process, for which detailed rules of procedure are authorized by the Measure. The findings of the tribunal must be announced in public.

6. It is the duty of the tribunal to report whether in its opinion there has been a serious breakdown of pastoral relationships, and whether the breakdown is one to which the conduct of the incumbent or the parishioners or both has contributed over a substantial period. The report must include recommendations as to the action to be taken by the bishop.

7. If, but only if, the tribunal so recommends, the bishop will execute a declaration declaring the benefice vacant as from a date not less than three or more than six months after the date of the declaration. Pending that date, the incumbent is disqualified from exercising any of the functions connected with the benefice without the consent of the bishop, and the bishop will make such other provision as he thinks fit for the performance of those functions. The Measure provides, in such a case, for

compensation to the incumbent for the loss of his office and for consequential expenses.

8. If the tribunal, though without making a recommendation for the vacation of the benefice, attributes blame to the incumbent for the breakdown, the bishop may rebuke the incumbent, and also has power of disqualification for such period as may be specified (other provision being made as above).

9. If the tribunal attributes blame to the parishioners, the bishop may rebuke such of the parishioners as he thinks fit, and in his discretion disqualify them from being churchwardens, or members or officers of a parochial church council. The disqualification, which is for a maximum term of five years, applies to such parish or parishes in the diocese as the bishop specifies.

10. Alternatively to reporting in accordance with (6) above, the tribunal may report that the incumbent is unable by reason of age or infirmity to discharge his or her duties adequately, with appropriate recommendations, and if it so reports, the same results will follow as if the inquiry had originally been directed to that matter (see below).

11. At any time before the bishop notifies the incumbent of the action to be taken as a result of the inquiry, the incumbent may voluntarily resign the benefice with the bishop's consent, in which event the same right to compensation arises as is mentioned in (7) above.

An inquiry on the ground of an incumbent's incapacity, arising from age or infirmity, can only be instituted on the bishop's own instructions. It is conducted by a provincial tribunal according to the same rules of procedure as are mentioned above. It is the duty of the tribunal to report whether, in its opinion, the incumbent is unable by reason of age or infirmity of mind or body to discharge adequately the duties attaching to the benefice, and, if so, to make recommendations as to the action to be taken by the bishop. If, but only if, the committee so recommends, the bishop may notify the incumbent that it is desirable that he or she should resign and if the incumbent then refuses to do so, the bishop must declare the benefice vacant. Other powers vested in the bishop, if the committee makes a positive report, are to appoint an assistant curate with the incumbent's consent, or to give the incumbent leave of absence not exceeding two years (making provision for the discharge of the incumbent's duties during that period); or to make other temporary provision for the discharge of the incumbent's duties. If the incumbent, having been requested to do so, does not consent to the appointment of an assistant curate, the bishop must declare the benefice vacant. If the benefice is vacated under any of the above-mentioned provisions, the incumbent is accorded special pension rights.

Avoidance of benefice

When an incumbent ceases to serve the duties of the cure, this is said to be an 'avoidance of the benefice'. This may occur by death, resignation, exchange, cession or deprivation, or by compulsory retirement on the ground of age, or by a declaration by the bishop under the Incumbents (Vacation of Benefices) Measure 1977. It also occurs if a sequestration of the profits of the benefice, consequent upon the incumbent's non-residence, continues for a full year, during the continued absence of the incumbent.

Exchange and cession

In order to effect an exchange the incumbents must obtain the consent of the respective patrons and diocesan bishops. Cession takes place when an incumbent is created a diocesan bishop, or is appointed to another benefice or preferment which cannot lawfully be held with the existing benefice (in this connection, the Pastoral Measure 1983 provides that, in general, no person can hold benefices in plurality except in pursuance of a pastoral scheme or order, and that no person can hold a cathedral preferment with a benefice unless the cathedral statutes so provide or allow).

Deprivation

Deprivation takes effect where there has been simony in connection with the presentation, institution, collation or admission to the benefice, whether the incumbent was or was not a party thereto, or where the incumbent was disqualified from holding the benefice, or by a censure of deprivation (as described in Chapter 2) for an offence by the incumbent.

Retirement

A compulsory retirement age for incumbents and for certain other other office-holders (including archbishops, diocesan and suffragan bishops, archdeacons, vicars in team ministries and vicars of guild churches) was imposed for the first time by the Ecclesiastical Offices (Age Limit) Measure 1975. Under this Measure, any office-holder to whom it applies is normally compelled to vacate office on attaining the age of 70, but in the case of an incumbent the bishop of the diocese may, on grounds of pastoral need, and with the consent of the parochial church council or councils concerned, from time to time authorize the incumbent's continuance in office for any extended period or periods not exceeding two years in all (so that the retiring age for an incumbent who is granted the maximum extension is 72). The Measure does not apply to any office-holder in respect of an office which he already held on 1st January 1976 (on which date the Measure came into force).[1]

Death

An incumbent ceases to have any rights to the emoluments of the benefice on the date when the incumbency ceases. When, however, an incumbent dies and there is a parsonage house attached to the benefice, a surviving spouse may continue to reside in the house for two calendar months.

Sequestrations

When a vacancy occurs in a benefice a process of sequestration is normally issued by the bishop, and some description of this process may therefore not be considered out of place here. Under it, the income of the benefice is ordered to be taken by the sequestrators and applied by them in a manner required by the circumstances of the case. There may be a sequestration when a benefice becomes vacant, or in certain other cases.[2]

In the case of a vacancy the normal practice is to appoint as

---

1 Where a person is designated by a pastoral scheme or order as the holder of an office, who was on 1st January 1976 the incumbent of a benefice affected by the scheme or order, and who continued so to be until the coming into operation of the scheme or order, he is to be deemed (in effect) to have held the designated office continuously from 1st January 1976 inclusive, and thus to be exempted from compulsory retirement: Church of England (Miscellaneous Provisions) Measure 1978, s. 2.

2 For other examples, see pp. 12 and 35 *et seq.*

sequestrators the churchwardens, the rural dean, and any other person whom the bishop may select. Where there is a team ministry the remaining ministers of the team act in place of the rural dean.

Until the coming into force of the Endowments and Glebe Measure 1976, the income receivable by the sequestrators included the income of the endowments of the benefice and of the glebe land (if any) belonging to it. But the effect of the Measure has been, in general, to substitute for these former sources of an incumbent's income a fixed annuity, which ceases to be payable during a vacancy in the benefice. In the result, apart from a few exceptional cases, the income of the benefice coming to the sequestrators during a vacancy will normally consist only of the marriage, burial and other fees which would have been payable to the incumbent if there had been one. In so far as these items are insufficient to meet the sequestrators' expenses, such expenses will be defrayed out of the diocesan stipends fund. Subject as mentioned below in the case of a benefice the right of presentation to which has been suspended, the sequestrators, at the close of the sequestration, will pay any balance in their hands, as certified by the bishop or some person authorized by him, to the Diocesan Board of Finance for allocation to the income account of the diocesan stipends fund.

If there is in the parish a licensed assistant curate at the time when the vacancy occurs, he or she continues in office. If there is no assistant curate, or if the assistant curate is unable alone to perform all the duties of the cure, the bishop may appoint a priest-in-charge to minister during the vacancy; the sequestrators may themselves employ and pay clergy for the purpose if the bishop does not act.

When the right of presentation to a benefice is in suspense (see pp. 50–1), the Pastoral Measure 1983, s. 68 and Schedule 7, makes the following special provisions about sequestration:

1. A process of sequestration must issue to cover the whole of the period of suspension, and the bishop must ensure that one of the sequestrators whom he appoints is specially qualified by training or experience to discharge the duties efficiently.
2. If the period of suspension immediately follows a period when the benefice has been vacant, any sequestrators appointed during the vacancy are to pay over any balance in their hands to the sequestrators appointed for the period of suspension.
3. The last-mentioned sequestrators must at the close of the sequestration, or from time to time during the sequestration,

account for any balance in their hands to the Church Commissioners; such balance must be allocated by the Commissioners to the income account of the diocesan stipends fund.

THE UNBENEFICED CLERGY

Generally

Every person in holy orders who does not hold a benefice is said to be 'unbeneficed'. There are many such persons (e.g. retired clergy and clergy in full-time teaching or administrative posts) who have no parochial responsibilities of their own. Clergy in this position may (and frequently do) hold the bishop's licence or permission to officiate in the diocese in which they live, and if so, they may properly be invited to officiate in any church in the diocese where help is needed.

But the unbeneficed clergy with which this book is chiefly concerned are those who are formally attached to specific parishes or benefices. They fall into two classes: first, ministers in charge of benefices which for the time being lack the services of any incumbent (generally called 'curates-in-charge' or 'priests-in-charge'); and secondly assistant curates – clergy appointed to assist incumbents within their parishes. It should be noted that neither of these classes of clergy are affected by the Ecclesiastical Offices (Age Limit) Measure 1975; thus there is no age limit either on their appointment or on their tenure of office.

Before considering these two classes in detail, some explanation may be useful of the expressions 'curate', 'assistant curate', 'curate-in-charge' and 'priest-in-charge', which can give rise to confusion:

1. 'Curate', in its strict and original sense, signified a priest who had the 'cure' or care of a parish, i.e. the incumbent or other minister in charge; the word has this meaning (for example) in the rubrics of the Prayer Book. An ordained person whose function is to assist the 'curate' (in the strict sense) is properly not a 'curate', but an 'assistant curate'.
2. Nevertheless, the practice of referring to an assistant curate simply as a 'curate', though historically and etymologically inaccurate, is now so universal that this has become the normally accepted meaning of the word: so much so that to use the word 'curate' of a clerk in holy orders holding any other position may be misleading.

3. It is incorrect to refer to an assistant curate, informally attached by the incumbent to a chapel-of-ease, as the 'curate-in-charge'; this is a mere matter of arrangement of duties within the parish, and the legal status of the assistant curate is unaffected. But 'curate-in-charge' is a correct description of an unbeneficed clerk formally appointed to the charge of a benefice in the incumbent's absence or where there is no incumbent; 'priest-in-charge' is an equally accurate description.

4. 'Curate-in-charge' is also the proper description of an assistant curate of a parish who has been given the care of a conventional district within the parish (see p. 25). Because of this other meaning of 'curate-in-charge', and also because the word 'curate' as applied to anyone not an assistant curate can give a wrong impression, it is preferable (as has been done in this book) to use the alternative description 'priest-in-charge' for an unbeneficed clerk in holy orders who has been appointed to the charge of a benefice.

Priests-in-charge

Whenever a benefice is under sequestration, the bishop has power to license a minister to be the priest-in-charge of the benefice for so long as the sequestration continues. There are various circum-stances in which a sequestration may occur (see for example pp. 35–8), but by far the most usual case is when a benefice becomes vacant. As soon as the vacancy occurs, a sequestration warrant is normally issued; the sequestration then commences, and the power to appoint a priest-in-charge becomes exercisable.

It is not, however, usually considered necessary to license a priest-in-charge for the comparatively short interval which normally elapses between the vacation of a benefice by one incum-bent and the admission of the next. In recent years appointments of priests-in-charge have become much more common than formerly, partly because it sometimes takes time to find a suitable new incumbent owing to a shortage of clergy, but principally because of the increasing exercise by diocesan bishops of their power under section 67 of the Pastoral Measure 1983 to suspend presentations to benefices (see pp. 50–1); this power is frequently made use of pending the formulation and bringing into operation of a pastoral scheme for reorganizing the benefices and parishes within a par-ticular area, and as a result of its exercise a benefice may well remain vacant over a period of years. In such a case, the appointment of a priest-in-charge is appropriate.

Before being licensed to a benefice, a priest-in-charge takes the oath of canonical obedience to the bishop and makes the declaration of assent (see p. 30) before the bishop or his commissary. And on the first Sunday on which the priest-in-charge officiates, the declaration of assent must be made in the church or one of the churches to which the licence extends in the presence of the congregation.

In general, a priest-in-charge has the same duties as an incumbent; and many of the Acts and Measures relating to the functions and duties of an incumbent extend to priests-in-charge by express definition. In particular, a priest-in-charge is in the same position as an incumbent as regards the convening and chairing of meetings of parishioners (for the appointment of churchwardens), of parochial church meetings, and of meetings of the parochial church council, and also for various other purposes such as the provisions of the Church of England (Worship and Doctrine) Measure 1974 and the canons thereunder.

Under the Pastoral Measure 1983, section 68(3), a priest-in-charge appointed for any benefice the presentation to which is suspended, may be required by the bishop to reside in the parsonage house. But unless this power is applicable and is actually exercised, a priest-in-charge is not under any obligation to reside in any particular house or within the area of the benefice.

A priest-in-charge's appointment, if not previously determined, will continue so long as the benefice continues to exist and remains under sequestration. But the licence of a priest-in-charge may be withdrawn at any time by the bishop (subject to a right of appeal to the archbishop of the province) after the priest-in-charge has been given an opportunity of being heard. If the priest-in-charge wishes to resign, three months' written notice must be given in advance to the bishop, unless the bishop waives this requirement.

There is no legal objection to a priest being licensed as priest-in-charge to any number of benefices, nor to an incumbent of one benefice being licensed as priest-in-charge of another benefice.

Assistant curates

The most usual reason for appointing one or more assistant curates to a parish is that the work of the parish is too heavy for a single-handed incumbent.

If not newly ordained to a parish, an assistant curate sometimes comes to it for a short time on trial at the invitation of the incumbent with the permission of the bishop. During this period there is no security of tenure and the assistant curate may be dismissed at the pleasure of the incumbent. In order to gain security, an assistant curate needs to be licensed to the curacy by the bishop who must be satisfied of the candidate's personal fitness. In order to be licensed the proposed assistant curate must be nominated by the incumbent of the parish, and if coming from another diocese the candidate is required to produce to the bishop a testimonial from the bishop of the diocese in which he or she was last licensed.

The licence granted to an assistant curate is an instrument under the seal of the bishop, which thereby confers a security of tenure in the curacy. The licence may be withdrawn at any time by the bishop after he has given the assistant curate an opportunity of being heard, and subject to a right of appeal by the assistant curate to the archbishop of the province. After the licence has been issued, the incumbent has a power to determine on six months' notice the appointment of the assistant curate; but this power may only be exercised with the bishop's consent. A parochial church council, as well as an incumbent, may complain to the bishop about the conduct of an assistant curate, and the churchwardens can make a presentment to the archdeacon or the bishop at the visitation.

The assistant curate may, on the other hand, resign on giving three months' notice to the incumbent and to the bishop, and in practice it is usual, if any complaint is proposed to be made to higher authority, to give an assistant curate the choice of resignation, unless the grounds of complaint are such as to constitute a scandal. The bishop has power to waive the requirement of notice.

Although the licence granted to an assistant curate usually has no time limit, the bishop now has power to grant such a licence for a specified term of years, at the end of which, if still on foot, it will expire unless renewed. During the specified term, the curate has the same security of tenure, subject to the same conditions, as under an indefinite licence.

On being licensed the assistant curate takes the oath of canonical obedience to the bishop. A declaration of assent[1] before the bishop or a commissary is also required, unless it has already been

---

1   See p. 30.

made at ordination on the same day. And on the first Sunday upon which the new assistant curate officiates in the church or one of the churches of the parish, the declaration of assent must be made in the presence of the congregation. It is desirable that this should be done in the parish church so that the churchwardens may certify the fact.

Copies of all licences to assistant curates are sent to the church-wardens for safe custody in the parish chest.

MEMBERS OF TEAM AND GROUP MINISTRIES

In the context of a team ministry, the words 'rector' and 'vicar' are used in special senses quite different from their traditional meanings.

The incumbent of the benefice or benefices to which a team ministry extends is always styled 'rector'. This office may be either a perpetual or 'freehold' office (as in the case of an incumbent of an ordinary benefice) or it may be limited by the pastoral scheme establishing the team ministry to a term of years only, with security of tenure during that term.[1]

The other members of the ministry are styled 'vicars', and the office of vicar must be limited to a specified term of years, with security of tenure during that term.[2] Vicars are chosen by the rector and the bishop jointly. They are appointed by licence of the bishop and publicly admitted in a church in the area of the team ministry.

Under the Ecclesiastical Offices (Age Limit) Measure 1975, vicars in team ministries, if appointed on or after 1st January 1976, are subject to the same rules as incumbents as to age on appoint-ment and as to compulsory retirement at the age of 70 or upwards (see pp. 29 and 38–9).

The rector is the leader of the team, and has a general responsi-bility for the cure of souls in the area. But there is power for the pastoral scheme or, subject to the scheme, for the bishop's licence

---

1   The Team and Group Ministries Measure 1995 now limits a team rector's appointment to a term of years only. Existing appointments, unlimited in time, are not affected retrospectively.

2   The Team and Group Ministries Measure 1995 also enables deacons to serve under licence for a term of years within a team ministry. The Ecclesi-astical Offices (Age Limit) Measure 1975 applies to them as it does to vicars.

appointing any vicar, to assign to such vicar a special cure of souls in respect of part of the area, or a special responsibility for a particular pastoral function, and further to provide that the special cure or responsibility shall be independent of the rector's general responsibility; and the rector's general responsibility is subject to any special cure or responsibility given to a vicar under these powers. There is also power for the scheme or the licence to assign to a vicar a general responsibility to be shared with the rector for the cure of souls in the area as a whole.

Apart from any exercise of the above-mentioned powers, a vicar, by virtue of office but subject to the licence, has authority to perform in the area of the team ministry all such offices and services as may be performed by an incumbent.

A group ministry is an association of incumbents, whose benefices are grouped together to form the area of the ministry. Each incumbent has authority to perform, in the area of every benefice within the group, all such offices and services as may be performed by the incumbent of that benefice; and all the incumbents are under a duty to assist each other, so as to make the best possible provision for the cure of souls throughout the area of the group ministry. But each incumbent, when operating in the area of a benefice within another incumbency, is bound to comply with the directions of the incumbent of that other benefice.

So long as any benefice is included in a group ministry its incumbent cannot resign from the group without also resigning the benefice.

The special provisions contained in the Pastoral Measure 1983 concerning parochial church meetings and councils, and district church councils, and group councils, within the areas of team and group ministries, include provisions conferring either membership of those bodies, or rights of attendance, on all the clergy participating in any such ministry. The text of the provisions in question is set out in Chapter 10.[1]

---

1   See p. 151.

ORDAINED WOMEN

In 1993 the Church of England took a major step by enabling women to be ordained to the priesthood. Previously a woman might only have been ordained deacon by virtue of the Deacons (Ordination of Women) Measure 1986 and Canon C4A made under the authority of that Measure. The legal effect of section 1 of the Priests (Ordination of Women) Measure 1993 and Canon C4B has simply been to remove the impediment which otherwise precluded a woman from becoming a priest. Following her ordination as a priest, a woman has precisely the same rights and obligations under ecclesiastical law as her male counterpart.

There is preserved at diocesan and at parochial level a power to restrict or exclude the ministry of women priests (but not women deacons). Within a parish, the parochial church council may for this purpose pass either or both of the following resolutions:

A. 'That this parochial church council would not accept a woman as the minister who presides at or celebrates the Holy Communion or pronounces absolution in the parish.'
B. 'That this parochial church council would not accept a woman as the incumbent or priest-in-charge of the benefice or as a team vicar for the benefice.'

In order to comply with the Measure there should be no departure from the wording of the resolutions as set out above. Unless there is a vacancy in the benefice, at least four weeks' prior notice has to be given of the meeting at which the proposed resolution is to be considered. A quorum of half the members of the council must attend the meeting. The same safeguards concerning notice and attendance apply to a motion to rescind the resolution; but subject to them the council may pass or rescind either or both of the resolutions on any number of occasions.

Notification must be given to the bishop, the rural dean, the lay chairman of the deanery synod, the diocesan registrar, the diocesan officer designated under section 7(5) of the Patronage (Benefices) Measure 1986 (see p. 51) and the registered patron of the benefice. No person (for example the diocesan bishop or the patron) may act in contravention of resolution A or resolution B while it remains in force in a parish. Similar restrictions apply to exclude the ministry of women priests in a diocese where the bishop has made the appropriate declaration, so that an individual parochial church council cannot override an exclusion imposed by the diocesan bishop. There is, however, one minor exception: the bishop's declaration does not prevent a woman from officiating as a priest in a church or chapel for one period of not more than seven days in any period of three months.

6 The Patron and Patronage

The right to present or appoint a person to a benefice is known as the 'right of patronage', and if the right is perpetual it is known as an 'advowson'. The person in whom the right is vested is called the 'patron'. The origin of ecclesiastical patronage is ancient and obscure, but it probably grew up gradually as an incident of the system by which, if a lord founded a church on his demesne, he acquired the right of patronage as the usual consequence.

The old law concerning patronage has been substantially altered by the Patronage (Benefices) Measure 1986. Of particular importance is the current procedure for the exercise of rights of presentation to a benefice, in which the parochial church council is involved as well as the patron and the bishop. The provisions of the Measure setting out this procedure are printed in the next section of the chapter.

The right of patronage is a form of property which the owner is freely entitled to deal with, subject to certain legal restrictions. An advowson may be transmitted by will. The Patronage (Benefices) Measure 1986, reflecting earlier repealed legislation, declares that a right of patronage is incapable of being sold and any attempt to transfer it for valuable consideration is void. New rights of patronage created under the Pastoral Measure 1983 or the enactments which preceded it are likewise, by express provision, unsaleable.

The Patronage (Benefices) Measure 1986 requires a register to be kept in each diocesan registry of the patrons of all the benefices within the diocese. Under the Measure, notice must be given to the bishop and the diocesan registrar of any proposal to transfer a right of patronage. The bishop's consent to the intended transfer is necessary, but before his consent may be given the parochial church council concerned is allowed one month to make representations. Unless an application for registration is made within twelve months of the date of the execution of the instrument of transfer, it has no effect in law. The personal representatives of a deceased patron do not, however, have to register their interest. They may exercise the right of patronage in place of the deceased if a presentation is to be made while the right is vested in them.

Where the patronage of a benefice belongs to an infant beneficially, the legal right to it is vested in trustees who instead make the presentation. If and so long as a patron is a person of unsound mind the right of presentation passes to the Crown.

The patron of a benefice may be a private person, or any other person or corporation recognized by law, for example the Crown, the Lord Chancellor, the diocesan bishop, a university, or a body of trustees. Section 10 of the Church of England (Miscellaneous Provisions) Measure 1992 confirmed that a parochial church council has itself power to hold and exercise a right of patronage. Every diocese has a diocesan board of patronage with a mixed clerical and lay membership, which exists for the purpose of acquiring and exercising rights of patronage.

When a new benefice is created (by union or otherwise) under a pastoral scheme, the scheme can make whatever provision is thought fit as to the patronage thereof (though regard is to be had to the interests of former patrons whose rights have been extinguished by the scheme); if no express provision is made, the diocesan board of patronage will be the patron. When a pastoral scheme creates a team ministry, the scheme itself may designate the first 'rector'; subject to any such designation, and so long as the team ministry continues, the right of patronage will be exercised either by the bishop (if he was originally the sole patron of the benefice), or (in any other case) by the diocesan board of patronage or a specially constituted board as the scheme may provide. In the case of a group ministry, existing rights of patronage in respect of benefices included in the group are not disturbed, but so long as the group ministry continues, a patron may not exercise any right of presentation without the bishop's approval of the person presented.

If no presentation is made within nine months of the vacancy, the right of presentation passes to the archbishop of the province. Neglect of this kind only affects the patron's right of presentation for that turn, and the general right of patronage remains in the patron.

Under section 67 of the Pastoral Measure 1983, the bishop may, in the case of a vacant benefice or one which is shortly to become vacant, with the consent of the pastoral committee and after consultation with the patron and with the parochial church council concerned, give notice that, for a period of not more than five years, the patron is not to exercise the right of presentation without the consent of the pastoral committee and the bishop. The period of suspension may thereafter be extended an indefinite number of times, by notice served by the bishop, with the same consent and after the same consultation, from time to time before each current period of suspension expires; but the period is not to be extended for more than five years by any one such notice.

During any period of suspension, there is a sequestration of the profits of the benefice (as to which see p. 39).

PATRONAGE (BENEFICES) MEASURE 1986 (SO FAR AS RELATING TO THE EXERCISE OF RIGHTS OF PRESENTATION) WITH NOTES

Notification of vacancies

7. (1) Subject to section 70 of the Pastoral Measure 1983,[1] where a benefice becomes vacant by reason of the death of the incumbent, the bishop shall, as soon as practicable after he becomes aware of the vacancy, give notice of that fact to the designated officer of the diocese.

   (2) Subject to section 70 of the Pastoral Measure 1983,[1] where the bishop is aware that a benefice is shortly to become vacant by reason of resignation or cession,[2] the bishop shall give such notice of that fact as he considers reasonable in all the circumstances to the designated officer of the diocese.

   (3) Any notice required to be given to the designated officer under subsection (1) or (2) above shall also be given to the registrar of the diocese, unless he is the designated officer.

   (4) As soon as practicable after receiving a notice under subsection (1) or (2) above the designated officer shall send notice of the vacancy to the registered patron of the benefice and to the secretary of the parochial church council of the parish belonging to the benefice; and any such notice shall include such information as may be prescribed.

   (5) In this Measure 'the designated officer', in relation to a diocese, means such person as the bishop, after consulting the bishop's council, may designate or, if no person is designated, the secretary of the pastoral committee of the diocese.

---

1 Section 70 provides that this procedure is not to be adopted where the right of presentation has been suspended or restricted in accordance with the Pastoral Measure 1983.

2 A vacancy by cession occurs when the incumbent becomes a diocesan bishop or obtains another preferment which cannot be held with the benefice.

Provisions as to declarations of membership

8. (1) Where the registered patron of a benefice is an individual and is not a clerk in Holy Orders, he shall on receiving notice of a vacancy in the benefice under section 7(4) of this Measure –

   (a) if able to do so, make a written declaration (in this Measure referred to as 'the declaration of membership') declaring that he is an actual communicant member of the Church of England or of a Church in communion with that Church; or

   (b) if unable to make the declaration himself, appoint some other person, being an individual who is able and willing to make it or is a clerk in Holy Orders or one of the bodies mentioned in subsection (7) below, to act as his representative to discharge in his place the functions of a registered patron.[1]

   (2) Where the registered patron of a benefice is a body of persons corporate or unincorporate then, on receiving notice of a vacancy in the benefice under section 7(4) of this Measure, that body shall appoint an individual who is able and willing to make the declaration of membership or is a clerk in Holy Orders to act as its representative to discharge in its place the functions of a registered patron.

   (3) Notwithstanding anything in subsection (1) above, where the registered patron of a benefice who is an individual and is not the bishop of a diocese is of the opinion, on receiving notice of a vacancy in the benefice under section 7(4) of this Measure, that he will be unable for any reason to discharge his functions as a patron of that benefice he may, notwithstanding that he is able to make the declaration of membership, appoint such a representative as is mentioned in subsection (1) (b) above to discharge those functions in his place.

   (4) Where a benefice the right of presentation to which belongs to an office (other than an ecclesiastical office) becomes vacant, the person who holds that office on the date on which the benefice becomes vacant shall be

---

1 This provision replaces the old disqualification affecting Roman Catholics; it applies generally to patrons who are not members of the Church of England.

entitled to present on that vacancy and shall as soon as practicable after that date –

    (a)   if able to do so, make the declaration of membership, or

    (b)   if unable to make the declaration himself, appoint some other person, being a person who may be appointed as a representative under subsection (1) (b) above, to act as his representative to discharge in his place the functions of a registered patron.

(5)   Where the right of presentation to a benefice is exercisable by the donee of a power of attorney,[1] the donee shall as soon as practicable after receiving notice of the vacancy in the benefice (or, if the power is created during the vacancy, as soon as practicable after it is created) –

    (a)   if able to do so, make the declaration of membership, or

    (b)   if unable to make the declaration himself, appoint some other person, being a person who may be appointed as a representative under subsection (1) (b) above, to act as his representative to discharge in his place the functions of a registered patron.

(6)   Where under the preceding provisions of this section a body mentioned in subsection (7) below is appointed to discharge the functions of a registered patron, that body shall as soon as practicable after being so appointed appoint as its representative an individual who is able and willing to make the declaration of membership or is a clerk in Holy Orders.

(7)   The bodies referred to in subsection (1) (b) above are –

    (a)   the dean and chapter or the cathedral chapter of the cathedral church of the diocese;

    (b)   the dean and chapter of the collegiate church of St Peter in Westminster;

    (c)   the dean and canons of the collegiate church of St George, Windsor;

    (d)   any diocesan board of patronage;

    (e)   any patronage board constituted by a pastoral scheme;

---

1   A power of attorney is a written instrument whereby a person authorizes another (the donee) to act on his behalf.

(f) any university in England or any college or hall in such a university; and

(g) the colleges of Eton and Winchester.

Information to be sent to designated officer

9. (1) Before the expiration of the period of two months beginning with the date on which a benefice becomes vacant or the expiration of three weeks after receiving notice of the vacancy from the designated officer under section 7(4) of this Measure, whichever is later,[1] a registered patron who is an individual shall send to the designated officer of the diocese –

(a) the declaration of membership made by him, or

(b) the name and address of his representative and the declaration of membership made by that representative.

(2) Before the expiration of the said period of two months or three weeks as the case may be, a registered patron which is a body of persons corporate or unincorporate shall send to the designated officer of the diocese the name and address of the individual who is to act as its representative and the declaration of membership made by that representative.

(3) Where the functions of a registered patron are to be discharged by the holder of an office, subsection (1) above shall apply to the person who holds that office on the date on which the benefice becomes vacant as it applies to the registered patron.

(4) Where the functions of a registered patron are to be discharged by the donee of a power of attorney, subsection (1) above shall apply to the donee as it applies to the registered patron except that, if the power is created during the vacancy concerned, there shall be substituted for the period of two months mentioned in that subsection the period of two months beginning with the date on which the power is created, and the information required to be sent under that subsection shall include information as to that date.

(5) Where the registered patron or his representative is a clerk in Holy Orders, the registered patron shall, before the expiration of the period during which the declaration of membership is required to be sent to the designated

---

1 The purpose of this amendment to the original Measure is to ensure that the patron is not disadvantaged by a delay in notice of the vacancy being given.

officer under the preceding provisions of this section, notify the designated officer of that fact, and a declaration of membership made by that clerk shall not be required to be sent to the designated officer under this section.

(6) As soon as practicable after receiving information under this section as to the appointment of a representative, the designated officer shall send to the secretary of the parochial church council the name and address of that representative.

Disqualification for presentation

10. Where the registered patron of a benefice or the representative of that patron, is a clerk in Holy Orders or is the wife of such a clerk, that clerk shall be disqualified for presentation to that benefice.[1]

Requirements as to meetings of parochial church council

11. (1) Before the expiration of the period of four weeks beginning with the date on which the notice under section 7(4) of this Measure is sent to the secretary of the parochial church council, one or more meetings of that council shall be held for the purposes of –

(a) preparing a statement describing the conditions, needs and traditions of the parish;[2]

(b) appointing two lay members of the council to act as representatives of the council in connection with the selection of an incumbent;

(c) deciding whether to request the registered patron to consider advertising the vacancy;

(d) deciding whether to request a meeting under section 12 of this Measure;

(e) deciding whether to request a statement in writing from the bishop describing in relation to the benefice the needs of the diocese and the wider interests of the Church; and

(f) deciding whether to pass a resolution under section 3(1) or (2) of the Priests (Ordination of Women) Measure 1993.[3]

---

1 The purpose of this provision is to prevent a priest from acquiring a benefice by obtaining direct control of the right of presentation to it.

2 There is no longer any prohibition against naming a particular clerk as a candidate for the vacancy.

3 See p. 47. The resolutions referred to would either declare a woman to be unacceptable as an incumbent, or would rescind an earlier resolution to that effect.

(2) A meeting of the parochial church council for which subsection (1) above provides shall be convened by the secretary thereof, and no member of that council who is –

    (a) the outgoing incumbent or the spouse[1] of the outgoing incumbent, or

    (b) the registered patron, or

    (c) the representative of the registered patron,

shall attend that meeting.

(3) None of the following members of the parochial church council, that is to say –

    (a) any person mentioned in subsection (2) above, and

    (b) any deaconess or lay worker licensed to the parish,

shall be qualified for appointment under subsection (1) (b) above.

(4) If before the vacancy in the benefice is filled any person appointed under subsection (1) (b) above dies or becomes unable for any reason to act as the representative of, or ceases to be a member of, the council by which he was appointed, then, except where he ceases to be such a member and the council decides that he shall continue to act as its representative, his appointment shall be deemed to have been revoked and the council shall appoint another lay member of the council (not being a member disqualified under subsection (3) above) to act in his place for the remainder of the proceedings under this Part of this Measure.

(5) If a parochial church council holds a meeting under subsection (1) above but does not appoint any representatives at that meeting, then, subject to subsection (6) below, two churchwardens who are members of that council (or, if there are more than two churchwardens who are members of the council, two churchwardens chosen by all the churchwardens who are members) shall act as representatives of the council in connection with the selection of an incumbent.

(6) A churchwarden who is the registered patron of a benefice shall not be qualified under subsection (5) above to act as a representative of the parochial church council

---

1 Under the usual rules of interpretation, this restriction also applies to the spouse of a female incumbent.

or to choose any other churchwarden so to act, and in any case where there is only one churchwarden qualified to act as such a representative that churchwarden may act as the sole representative of that council in connection with the selection of the incumbent.

(7) Any representative of the parochial church council appointed under subsection (1) to (4) above and any churchwarden acting as such a representative by virtue of subsection (5) or (6) above is in this Part of this Measure referred to as a 'parish representative', and where a churchwarden is entitled to act as the sole parish representative any reference in this Part to the parish representatives shall be construed as a reference to that churchwarden.

(8) A copy of the statement prepared under subsection (1) (a) above together with the names and addresses of the parish representatives shall, as soon as practicable after the holding of the meeting under that subsection, be sent by the secretary of the parochial church council, to the registered patron and, unless the bishop is the registered patron, to the bishop.

Joint meeting of parochial church council with bishop and patron

12. (1) Where a request for a meeting under this section is made –

    (a) by a notice sent by the registered patron or the bishop to the secretary of the parochial church council, or

    (b) by a resolution of the parochial church council, passed at a meeting held under section 11 of this Measure,

a joint meeting of the parochial church council with the registered patron and (if the bishop is not the registered patron) the bishop shall be held for the purpose of enabling those present at the meeting to exchange views on the statement prepared under section 11 (1)(a) of this Measure (needs of the parish) and the statement presented under subsection (2) below (needs of the diocese).

(2) At any meeting held under this section the bishop shall present either orally or, if a request for a statement in writing has been made by the registered patron or the parochial church council, in writing a statement describing

in relation to the benefice the needs of the diocese and the wider interests of the Church.

(3)   Any notice given under subsection (1)(a) above shall be of no effect unless it is sent to the secretary of the parochial church council not later than ten days after a copy of the statement prepared under subsection (1)(a) of section 11 of this Measure is received by the persons mentioned in subsection (8) of that section.

(4)   The outgoing incumbent and the spouse[1] of the outgoing incumbent shall not be entitled to attend a meeting held under this section.

(5)   A meeting requested under this section shall be held before the expiration of the period of six weeks beginning with the date on which the request for the meeting was first made (whether by the sending of a notice as mentioned in subsection (l)(a) above or by the passing of a resolution as mentioned in subsection (1) (b) above), and at least fourteen days' notice (unless a shorter period is agreed by all the persons concerned) of the time and place at which the meeting is to be held shall be given by the secretary of the parochial church council to the registered patron, the bishop (if he is not the registered patron) and the members of the parochial church council.

(6)   If either the registered patron or the bishop is unable to attend a meeting held under this section, he shall appoint some other person to attend on his behalf.

(7)   The chairman of any meeting held under this section shall be such person as the persons who are entitled to attend and are present at the meeting may determine.

(8)   No meeting requested under this section shall be treated for the purposes of this Measure as having been held unless there were present at the meeting –

(a)   the bishop or the person appointed by the bishop to attend on his behalf, and

(b)   the registered patron or the person appointed by the patron to attend on his behalf, and

(c)   at least one third of the members of the parochial church council who were entitled to attend.

---

1   The husband, where the incumbent is a woman.

(9) The secretary of the parochial church council shall invite both the rural dean of the deanery in which the parish is (unless he is the outgoing incumbent) and the lay chairman of the deanery synod of that deanery to attend a meeting held under this section.

Provisions with respect to selection of incumbent

13. (1) The registered patron of a vacant benefice shall not make to any priest an offer to present him to a benefice until –

    (a) if a request for a meeting under section 12 of this Measure has been made, either –

        (i) that meeting has been held, or

        (ii) all the parties concerned have agreed that no such meeting should be held, or

        (iii) the period of six weeks mentioned in section 12(5) has expired; and

    (b) (whether or not such a request has been made) the making of the offer to the priest in question has been approved –

        (i) by the parish representatives, and

        (ii) if the registered patron is a person other than the bishop of the diocese in which the benefice is, by that bishop.[1]

(2) If, before the expiration of the period of four weeks beginning with the date on which the registered patron sent to the bishop a request for him to approve under paragraph (b) of subsection (1) above the making of the offer to the priest named in the request, no notice is received from the bishop of his refusal to approve the making of the offer, the bishop shall be deemed to have given his approval under that paragraph.

(3) If, before the expiration of the period of two weeks beginning with the date on which the registered patron sent to the parish representatives a request for them to approve under paragraph (b) of subsection (1) above the making of the offer to the priest named in the request, no notice is received from any representative of his refusal to approve

---

1   The effect of this provision is that the bishop (if he is not the patron) or the parish representatives may override the patron's choice; but the patron has in those circumstances the right to appeal to the archbishop under subsection (5).

the making of the offer, the representatives shall be deemed to have given their approval under that paragraph.

(4) If –

(a) the bishop refuses to approve under paragraph (b) of subsection (1) above the making of the offer to the priest named in the request, or

(b) any parish representative refuses to approve under that paragraph the making of that offer,

the bishop or the representative, as the case may be, shall notify the registered patron in writing of the grounds on which the refusal is made.

(5) Where approval of an offer is refused under subsection (4) above, the registered patron may request the archbishop to review the matter and if, after review, the archbishop authorizes the registered patron to make the offer in question, the patron may make that offer accordingly. Provided that this subsection shall not apply in respect of –

(a) a parish in a diocese to which a declaration under section 2(1)(b) of the Priests (Ordination of Women) Measure 1993 applies; or

(b) a benefice comprising a parish to which a resolution under section 3(1) of that Measure applies,

where the refusal is made solely on grounds of gender.

(6) Where a priest accepts an offer made in accordance with the provisions of this section to present him to a benefice and the registered patron is a person other than the bishop, the patron shall send the bishop a notice presenting the priest to him for admission to the benefice.

Failure of registered patron to comply with section 9

14. (1) Where any declaration of membership or other information required to be sent to the designated officer under section 9 of this Measure is not sent to that officer before the expiration of the period during which it is required to be so sent and the registered patron is a person other than the bishop then, after the expiration of that period –

(a) no meeting shall be held under section 12 of this Measure by reason of any request made by the registered patron and subsections (2), (5), (6) and (8) of that section shall not apply in relation to that patron; and

(b) no offer shall be made to any priest under section 13 of this Measure;

but the bishop may, subject to subsection (2) below, make to such priest as he thinks fit an offer to collate him to the benefice.

(2) The bishop shall not make an offer under subsection (1) above unless the making of the offer has been approved by the parish representatives, and subsections (3), (4) (b) and (5) of section 13 of this Measure shall apply in relation to a request sent by the bishop to those representatives by virtue of this subsection as if for any reference to the registered patron there were substituted a reference to the bishop.

(3) Where under subsection (1) above the bishop makes to a priest an offer to collate him to a benefice in respect of which there is more than one person registered under this Measure, the registered patron whose turn it was to present to the benefice shall be treated for the purposes of this Measure as having exercised that turn.

Failure of council to comply with sections 11 or 12

15. If a copy of the statement prepared under section 11(1) (a) of this Measure is not sent under subsection (8) of that section to the persons mentioned in that subsection or if notice is not given under section 12(5) of this Measure of any joint meeting requested under subsection (1) (a) of the said section 12 then –

(a) if the bishop is the registered patron, he may, without making any request for the approval of the parish representatives, make to such priest as he thinks fit an offer to collate him to the benefice; and

(b) if the bishop is not the registered patron, that patron shall be entitled to proceed under section 13 of this Measure as if paragraphs (a) and (b)(i) of subsection (1), subsection (3) and paragraph (b) of subsection (4) thereof had not been enacted.

APPOINTING A NEW INCUMBENT

This table sets out the procedure under the Patronage (Benefices) Measure 1986 to be followed in a straightforward case.

Step	Provision in Measure	Time
(i) Bishop gives notice of vacancy to Registrar or other designated officer.	Section 7 (1), (2)	When vacancy occurs or is imminent.
(ii) Designated officer gives notice to (a) registered patron (b) PCC secretary.	Section 7 (4)	As soon as practicable after (i).
(iii) PCC meets to prepare statement under Section 11/ appoint parish representatives/ request first meeting.	Section 11 (1)	Within four weeks of notice at (ii).
(iv) Patron sends to designated officer declaration of membership or details of patron's representative.	Section 9	Within two months of vacancy or three weeks of (ii) whichever is later.
(v) Section 11 statement sent to bishop and patron with request for joint meeting if desired by PCC.	Section 11 (8)	As soon as practicable after (iii).
(vi) Patron or bishop request joint meeting.	Section 12 (2)	Within ten days of receiving section 11 statement.
(vii) Joint meeting between patron (or representative), bishop and PCC if requested under (v) or (vi).	Section 12	Within six weeks of request.
(viii) Patron requests approval of bishop and parish representatives to choice of priest.	Section 13	After joint meeting, if held; or expiration of six weeks after joint meeting requested but does not take place.
(ix) Making of offer approved by parish representatives.	Section 13 (3)	Within two weeks of request for approval.
(x) Making of offer approved by bishop.	Section 13 (2)	Within four weeks of request for approval.
(xi) Patron makes offer to present priest to benefice.	Section 13 (1)	After approvals under (ix) and (x) given, or no refusal to approve received by patron within time limits.
(xii) Priest accepts offer.	Section 13 (6)	Unspecified.
(xiii) Patron sends a notice to bishop presenting priest to benefice.	Section 13 (6)	Unspecified.

7 The Office of Churchwarden

The office of churchwarden is a venerable one, which had already emerged into legal recognition by the thirteenth century. Two centuries later the churchwardens were chosen annually in parish meeting, all adult parishioners having a voice in the election. Once elected, the churchwardens normally transacted all parish business during their year of office. They had, in fact, a twofold significance: they were both guardians of the parochial morals and trustees of the Church's goods.

The functions of churchwardens at the present time are dealt with in the next chapter of this book. This present chapter is concerned with their qualification and manner of appointment, and with the modes whereby the office of churchwarden may be vacated. The law on these subjects was first brought together in the Churchwardens (Appointment and Resignation) Measure 1964, which with minor amendment remained in force until its replacement in January 2002 by the Churchwardens Measure 2001. Much of the 1964 Measure is re-enacted in the new Measure, but there are some entirely fresh provisions, principally concerning the disqualification of churchwardens. Steps have also been taken to make the new legislation consistent with the Pastoral Measure 1983 and the Church Representation Rules as they now stand.

CHURCHWARDENS MEASURE 2001, WITH NOTES

A Measure passed by the General Synod of the Church of England to make fresh provision with respect to churchwardens in the Church of England.

Number and qualifications of churchwardens

1. (1) Subject to the provisions of this Measure there shall be two churchwardens of every parish.[1]

(2) (a) Where by virtue of a designation made by a pastoral scheme or otherwise a parish has more than one parish church, two churchwardens shall be appointed for each of the parish churches, and this Measure shall apply separately to each pair of churchwardens, but all the churchwardens shall be churchwardens of the whole parish, except so far as they may arrange to perform separate duties in relation to the several parish churches.[2]

(b) A church building or part of a building designated as a parish centre of worship under section 29(2) of the Pastoral Measure 1983, shall, subject to subsection (4) of that section,[3] be deemed while the designation is in force to be a parish church for the purposes of this subsection.

(3) The churchwardens[4] of every parish shall be chosen from persons who have been baptised and –

(a) whose names are on the church electoral roll of the parish;

(b) who are actual communicants,[5]

(c) who are twenty-one years of age or upwards; and

(d) who are not disqualified under section 2 or 3 below.

---

1 Exceptionally, there may be a different number by custom; see section 11(2) below. A further exception is made by section 1(2) where there is more than one place of worship within a parish.

2 This subsection previously appeared in section 27(5) of the Pastoral Measure 1983.

3 Subsection (4) simply prevents the designation from bringing the building automatically within the faculty jurisdiction.

4 The additional requirement of residence in the parish, which appeared in the Measure of 1964, has been removed. The effect of subsection (3) is to abrogate any surviving common law disqualification, such as was thought to affect Jews and those of foreign nationality. The only remaining disqualifications appear in sections 2 and 3.

5 The expression 'actual communicant' extends to a person permitted to receive Holy Communion who is not a member of the Church of England.

(4) If it appears to the bishop, in the case of any particular person who is not qualified by virtue of paragraph (a), (b) or (c) of subsection (3) above, that there are exceptional circumstances which justify a departure from the requirements of those paragraphs the bishop may permit that person to hold the office of churchwarden notwithstanding that those requirements are not met. Any such permission shall apply only to the period of office next following the date on which the permission is given.[1]

(5) No person shall be chosen as churchwarden of a parish for any period of office unless he –

(a) has signified consent to serve as such; or

(b) has not signified consent to serve as such for the same period of office in any other parish (not being a related parish) or, if such consent has been signified and the meeting of the parishioners to elect churchwardens of that other parish has been held, was not chosen as churchwarden of that other parish.[2]

In this subsection 'related parish' means a parish –

(i) belonging to the benefice to which the first-mentioned parish belongs; or

(ii) belonging to a benefice held in plurality with the benefice to which the first-mentioned parish belongs; or

(iii) having the same minister as the first-mentioned parish.

(6) In relation to the filling of a casual vacancy among the churchwardens the reference in subsection (5)(b) above to the same period of office shall be construed as a reference to a period of office which includes the period for which the casual vacancy is to be filled.

---

1   This provision enables a bishop to dispense, for a single term of a churchwarden's office, from the qualifications in subsection (3). The bishop's permission must be given before nomination; see section 4(4). The exceptional circumstances justifying this step are not defined, but include the absence in the parish of sufficient qualified persons consenting to serve.

2   The effect of these words is to prevent a churchwarden from serving as such in two unconnected parishes simultaneously. Procedurally this is achieved by disqualifying the candidate for so long as he or she has consented to serve in another parish, until the election has taken place in that parish and the candidate has not been chosen there. Subsection (6) applies the same rule to casual vacancies.

General disqualifications

2. (1) A person shall be disqualified from being chosen for the office of churchwarden if he is disqualified from being a charity trustee under section 72(1) of the Charities Act 1993[1] and the disqualification is not for the time being subject to a general waiver by the Charity Commissioners under subsection (4) of that section or to a waiver by them under that subsection in respect of all ecclesiastical charities established for the purposes related to the parish concerned.

   In this subsection 'ecclesiastical charity' has the same meaning as that assigned to that expression in the Local Government Act 1894.

   (2) (a) A person shall be disqualified from being chosen for the office of churchwarden if he has been convicted of any offence mentioned in Schedule 1 to the Children and Young Persons Act 1933.

   (b) In paragraph (a) above the reference to any offence mentioned in Schedule 1 to the Children and Young Persons Act 1933 shall include an offence which, by virtue of any enactment, is to be treated as being included in any such reference in all or any of the provisions of that Act.

   (3) A person shall be disqualified from being chosen for the office of churchwarden if he is disqualified from holding that office under section 10(6) of the Incumbents (Vacation of Benefices) Measure 1977.[2]

   (4) All rules of law whereby certain persons are disqualified from being chosen for the office of churchwarden shall cease to have effect.

Disqualification after six periods of office

3. Without prejudice to section 2 above, a person shall be disqualified from being chosen for the office of churchwarden when that person has served as a churchwarden of the same parish for six successive periods of office until the annual meeting of the parishioners to elect churchwardens in the next year but one

---

1   See p. 130 footnote 1.
2   See p. 130 footnote 2.

following the date on which that person vacated office at the end of the last such period:

Provided that a meeting of the parishioners may by resolution decide that this section shall not apply in relation to the parish concerned.

Any such resolution may be revoked by a subsequent meeting of the parishioners.[1]

Time and manner of choosing

4. (1) The churchwardens of a parish shall be chosen annually not later than 30th April in each year.

(2) Subject to the provisions of this Measure[2] the churchwardens of a parish shall be elected by a meeting of the parishioners.

(3) Candidates for election at the meeting must be nominated and seconded in writing by persons entitled to attend the meeting and each nomination paper must include a statement, signed by the person nominated, to the effect that that person is willing to serve as a churchwarden and is not disqualified under section 2(1), (2) or (3) above.[3]

(4) A nomination shall not be valid unless –

(a) the nomination paper is received by the minister of the parish before the commencement of the meeting; and

(b) in the case of a person who is not qualified by virtue of section 1(3)(a), (b) or (c) above, the bishop's permission was given under section 1(4) above

---

1   This limitation upon a churchwarden's length of service is entirely new. It imposes a mandatory space of two years during which a churchwarden who has served for six continuous periods of office cannot be re-elected until two years have elapsed. The meeting of the parishioners may, however, by a simple majority under section 5(6) resolve that the present disqualification shall not apply to the parish. The resolution may itself be rescinded by a similar majority at a later meeting. In any event section 3 will not take effect until six successive periods of office under the present Measure have been completed; periods served under the Churchwardens (Appointment and Resignation) Measure do not count (see Schedule 1, p. 77).

2   These words preserve existing custom for the selection of churchwardens; see section 11, p. 74.

3   There is no prescribed form of nomination paper, but a specimen is printed at p. 78.

before the nomination paper is received by the minister of the parish.

(5) If it appears to the minister of the parish that the election of any particular person nominated might give rise to serious difficulties between the minister and that person in the carrying out of their respective functions the minister may, before the election is conducted, make a statement to the effect that only one churchwarden is to be elected by the meeting. In that event one churchwarden shall be appointed by the minister from among the persons nominated, the name of the person so appointed being announced before the election is conducted, and the other shall then be elected by the meeting.[1]

(6) During any period when there is no minister –

(a) subsection (4) above shall apply with the substitution for the words 'minister of the parish' of the words 'churchwarden by whom the notice convening the meeting was signed'; and

(b) subsection (5) above shall not apply.

(7) A person may be chosen to fill a casual vacancy among the churchwardens at any time.

(8) Any person chosen to fill a casual vacancy shall be chosen in the same manner as was the churchwarden whose place he is to fill except that, where the churchwarden concerned was appointed by the minister and the minister has ceased to hold office, the new churchwarden to fill the casual vacancy shall be elected by a meeting of the parishioners.

---

1 This modified procedure replaces the old practice (embodied in section 2(3) of the Churchwardens (Appointment and Resignation) Measure 1964) whereby, in the event of disagreement between the minister and parishioners as to the choice of both churchwardens, one should be appointed by the minister and the other elected by the parishioners. The minister's power of appointment will now be limited to circumstances in which the minister expects 'serious difficulties' to result from the election of one of the persons nominated. Mere disagreement about the selection of the churchwardens is not enough. To exercise the right to appoint a churchwarden, the minister before the election must name the minister's appointee and make a statement that only one churchwarden is to be elected. There is no obligation to name the candidate to whom the minister takes objection.

Meeting of the parishioners

5. (1) A joint meeting of –

    (a) the persons whose names are entered on the church electoral roll of the parish; and

    (b) the persons resident in the parish whose names are entered on a register of local government electors by reason of such residence,

shall be deemed to be a meeting of the parishioners for the purposes of this Measure.

(2) The meeting of the parishioners shall be convened by the minister or, during any period when there is no minister or when the minister is unable or unwilling to do so, the churchwardens of the parish by a notice signed by the minister or a churchwarden as the case may be.

(3) The notice shall state the place, day and hour at which the meeting of the parishioners is to be held.

(4) The notice shall be affixed on or near to the principal door of the parish church and of every other building licensed for public worship in the parish for a period including the last two Sundays before the meeting.

(5) The minister, if present, or, if he is not present, a chairman chosen by the meeting of the parishioners, shall preside thereat.

(6) In case of an equal division of votes on any question other than one to determine an election of a churchwarden the chairman of the meeting of parishioners shall not have a second or casting vote and the motion on that question shall be treated as lost.

(7) The meeting of the parishioners shall have power to adjourn, and to determine its own rules of procedure.

(8) A person appointed by the meeting of the parishioners shall act as clerk of the meeting and shall record the minutes thereof.

Admission

6. (1) At a time and place to be appointed by the bishop annually, being on a date not later than 31st July in each year, each person chosen for the office of churchwarden shall appear before the bishop, or his substitute duly appointed, and be admitted to the office of churchwarden after –

(a) making a declaration, in the presence of the bishop or his substitute, that he will faithfully and diligently perform the duties of his office; and

(b) subscribing a declaration to that effect and also that he is not disqualified under section 2(1), (2) or (3) above.

No person chosen for the office of churchwarden shall become churchwarden until such time as he shall have been admitted to office in accordance with the provisions of this section.[1]

(2) Subject to the provisions of this Measure[2] the term of office of the churchwardens so chosen and admitted as aforesaid shall continue until a date determined as follows, that is to say –

(a) in the case of a person who is chosen again as churchwarden at the next annual meeting of the parishioners –

(i) if so admitted for the next term of office by 31st July in the year in question, the date of the admission; or

(ii) if not so admitted for the next term of office by 31st July in the year in question, that date;

---

1 The admission of churchwardens, after subscribing the declaration referred to in this subsection, ordinarily takes place at the annual 'visitation'. It is usual for a bishop to 'visit' the diocese from time to time. In the case of an episcopal visitation the admission takes place before the bishop or the chancellor or a surrogate. In other years it is performed at an archdeacon's visitation. It is open to any person to allege that some cause exists why the persons claiming admission should not be admitted to office; and the bishop or archdeacon, as the case may be, may make inquiries before admitting a person even if no such cause is alleged. But any refusal to admit a person as churchwarden must be on the ground of some definite legal disqualification (e.g. lack of due age, or disqualification from being a charity trustee or for some other reason mentioned in section 2 of this Measure) and not on any such ground as alleged unfitness for moral or other reasons. The remedy for a refusal to admit is by proceedings in the High Court of Justice.

It should be stressed that a newly appointed churchwarden is not in office until actually admitted. If prevented by illness or other good reason from attending the visitation, the person chosen may be admitted by arrangement before a surrogate.

2 A term of office settled by custom is thereby preserved. See section 13, p. 74.

(b) in the case of a person who is not chosen again as churchwarden at the next annual meeting of the parishioners –

    (i) if that person's successor in office is so admitted for the next term of office by 31st July in the year in question, the date of the admission; or

    (ii) if that person's successor in office is not so admitted for the next term of office by 31st July in the year in question, that date.

In the application of paragraph (b) above to any person, where there is doubt as to which of the new churchwardens is that person's successor in office the bishop may designate one of the new churchwardens as that person's successor for the purposes of that paragraph.

(3) Where any person ceases to hold the office of churchwarden at the end of July in any year by virtue of paragraph (a)(ii) or (b)(ii) above a casual vacancy in that office shall be deemed to have arisen.

(4) In relation to the filling of a casual vacancy the reference in subsection (1) above to 31st July shall be construed as a reference to a date three months after the person who is to fill the vacancy is chosen or the date of the next annual meeting of the parishioners to elect churchwardens, whichever is the earlier.

Resignation

7. (1) A person may resign the office of churchwarden in accordance with the following provisions of this section, but not otherwise.[1]

(2) Written notice of intention to resign shall be served on the bishop by post.

(3) The resignation shall have effect and the office shall be vacated –

    (a) at the end of the period of two months following service of the notice on the bishop; or

    (b) on such earlier date as may be determined by the

---

1 Previously the written consent of the minister was required. Under the present Measure, the only involvement of the minister is to consult with the bishop if it is proposed that the office of churchwarden shall be vacated within a shorter period than two months of notice being given.

bishop after consultation with the minister and any other churchwarden of the parish.

Vacation of office

8. (1) The office of churchwarden of a parish shall be vacated if –

    (a) the name of the person concerned is removed from the church electoral roll of the parish under rule 1 of the Church Representation Rules;[1] or

    (b) the name of the person concerned is not on a new church electoral roll of the parish prepared under rule 2(4) of those Rules; or

    (c) the churchwarden becomes disqualified under section 2(1), (2) or (3) above.[2]

(2) For the purposes of this section a person who has been chosen for the office of churchwarden but has not yet been admitted to that office shall be deemed to hold that office, and the expressions 'office' and 'churchwarden' shall be construed accordingly.

Guild churches

9. (1) In the case of every church in the City of London designated and established as a Guild Church under the City of London (Guild Churches) Acts 1952 and 1960 the churchwardens shall, notwithstanding anything to the contrary contained in those Acts, be actual communicant members of the Church of England except where the bishop shall otherwise permit.[3]

---

1 See p. 95 *et seq.*

2 Presumably the office will be vacated under this section when a ground for disqualification was not disclosed at the time of nomination but was discovered after the churchwarden has been admitted under section 6.

3 As to guild churches generally, see pp. 26–7. Under the Act of 1952, the churchwardens of a guild church (two in number) are chosen by the vicar and members of the guild church electoral roll at an annual guild church meeting held in each year before Low Sunday. Eligible candidates are persons who are either on the guild church electoral roll, or eligible to be churchwardens of some parish in the City of London.

(2) Subject to subsection (1) above, nothing in this Measure shall apply to the churchwardens of any church designated and established as a Guild Church under the City of London (Guild Churches) Acts 1952 and 1960.

(3) In this section 'actual communicant member of the Church of England' means a member of the Church of England who is confirmed or ready and desirous of being confirmed and has received Communion according to the use of the Church of England or of a church in communion with the Church of England at least three times during the twelve months preceding the date of his election or appointment.

Special provisions

10. (1) In the carrying out of the provisions of this Measure the bishop shall have power –

    (a) to make provision for any matter not herein provided for;

    (b) to appoint a person to do any act in respect of which there has been any neglect or default on the part of any person or body charged with any duty under this Measure;

    (c) so far as may be necessary for the purpose of giving effect to the intentions of this Measure, to extend or alter the time for holding any meeting or election or to modify the procedure laid down by this Measure in connection therewith;

    (d) in any case in which there has been no valid choice to direct a fresh choice to be made, and to give such directions in connection therewith as he may think necessary; and

    (e) in any case in which any difficulty arises, to give any directions which he may consider expedient for the purpose of removing the difficulty.

(2) The powers of the bishop under this section shall not enable him to validate anything that was invalid at the time it was done.

Savings

11. (1) Subject to section 9 above, nothing in this Measure shall be deemed to amend, repeal or affect any local act or any scheme made under any enactment affecting the churchwardens of a parish:

Provided that for the purposes of this Measure the Parish of Manchester Division Act 1850 shall be deemed to be a general act.

(2) Subject to section 12 below, in the case of any parish where there is an existing custom which regulates the number of churchwardens or the manner in which the churchwardens are chosen, nothing in this Measure shall affect that custom:[1]

Provided that in the case of any parish where in accordance with that custom any churchwarden was, before the coming into force of the Churchwardens (Appointment and Resignation) Measure 1964, chosen by the vestry of that parish jointly with any other person or persons that churchwarden shall be chosen by the meeting of the parishioners jointly with the other person or persons.

Abolition of existing customs

12. (1) A meeting of the parishioners of a parish may pass a resolution abolishing any existing custom which regulates the number of churchwardens of the parish or the manner in which the churchwardens of the parish are chosen.[2]

(2) Where any such resolution is passed the existing custom to which it relates shall cease to have effect on the date on which the next meeting of parishioners by which the churchwardens are to be elected is held.

---

1 Instances of local customs are numerous. There can be a valid custom whereby there may be only one churchwarden, or three or more churchwardens, for a parish; or whereby churchwardens are elected for separate parts of a parish. In most ancient parishes in the City of London, there is a custom whereby both churchwardens are chosen by the parishioners.

2 Under the law before the passing of the present Measure there was no method of abolishing a custom which had been observed since 1st January 1925. This section enables a custom to be replaced by the provisions of the Measure in relation to the number, and manner of selecting, churchwardens. Once a custom has been abolished, the Measure does not permit its revival by a later resolution of a meeting of the parishioners.

(3) In the case of an existing custom which involves a person other than the minister in the choice of the churchwardens, a resolution under subsection (1) above shall not be passed without the written consent of that person.

Interpretation

13. (1) In this Measure, except in so far as the context otherwise requires –

'bishop' means the diocesan bishop concerned;[1]

'existing custom' means a custom existing at the coming into force of this Measure which has continued for a period[2] commencing before 1st January 1925;

'minister' has the same meaning as that assigned to that expression in rule 54(1) of the Church Representation Rules[3] except that, where a special responsibility for pastoral care in respect of the parish in question has been assigned to a member of the team in a team ministry under section 20(8A) of the Pastoral Measure 1983 but a special cure of souls in respect of the parish has not been assigned to a vicar in the team ministry by a scheme under that Measure or by his licence from the bishop, it means that member;

'pastoral scheme' has the same meaning as that assigned to that expression in section 87(1) of the Pastoral Measure 1983;

'actual communicant', 'parish' and 'public worship' have the same meanings respectively as those assigned to those expressions in rule 54(1)[3] of the Church Representation Rules.

(2) Where by virtue of any custom existing at the coming into force of the Churchwardens (Appointment and

---

1   Section 10 of the Dioceses Measure 1978, however, permits a diocesan bishop's functions to be delegated to a suffragan bishop.
2   Although expressed differently, this is the same period of time specified in the Churchwardens (Appointment and Resignation) Measure 1964.
3   Page 134.

Resignation) Measure 1964 the choice of a church-warden was, under section 12(2) of that Measure, required to be made by the meeting of the parishioners jointly with another person or persons that custom shall be deemed to be an existing custom for the purposes of this Measure.

Transitional provisions

14. The transitional provisions in Schedule 1 to this Measure shall have effect.

15. ...[1]

Short title, commencement and extent

16. (1) This Measure may be cited as the Churchwardens Measure 2001.

(2) This Measure shall come into force on such day as the Archbishops of Canterbury and York appoint, and differ-ent days may be appointed for different provisions.[2]

(3) This Measure shall extend to the whole of the Provinces of Canterbury and York except the Channel Islands and the Isle of Man, but the provisions thereof may be applied to the Channel Islands as defined in the Channel Islands (Church Legislation) Measures 1931 and 1957, or either of them, in accordance with those Measures and if an Act of Tynwald or an instrument made in pursuance of an Act of Tynwald so provides, shall extend to the Isle of Man subject to such exceptions, adaptations or modifica-tions as may be specified in the Act of Tynwald or instru-ment.

---

1   Section 15 merely repealed certain previous enactments and it is unneces-sary to reproduce it here.
2   The whole Measure came into force on 1 January 2002.

SCHEDULE 1

Transitional provisions

1. Nothing in this Measure shall affect a churchwarden in office before the coming into force of this Measure during the period for which he was chosen.[1]
2. For the purposes of section 3 above no account shall be taken of any period of office commencing before the coming into force of this Measure.

Schedule 2 . . .
Schedule 3 . . . [2]

---

1   The Measure is prevented from having retrospective effect.
2   Schedules 2 and 3, concerning consequential amendments and repeals, are not printed here. It should, however, be noted that the whole of the churchwardens (Appointment and Resignation) Measure 1964 has been repealed.

SPECIMEN NOMINATION PAPER

(see section 4(3) printed at p. 67.
This is not a prescribed form, but may be found of use.)

Election of Churchwardens

We propose

(name) ....

(address) ....

....

for election to the office of a churchwarden in this parish during the term commencing in the year ....

Signed   (1) ....

(name in capitals) ....

Signed   (2) ....

(name in capitals) ....

Statement

1 .... the person nominated above, confirm that I am willing to serve as a churchwarden and that I am not disqualified from office on any of the grounds set out in sections 2(1), (2) or (3) of the Churchwardens Measure 2001.

Signed ....

8 The Functions of Churchwardens

CHURCHWARDENS AND CHAPELWARDENS

In this chapter it is proposed to consider the functions of church-wardens after their admission to office. These functions extend to every consecrated church and chapel within the parish. While it is usual to have wardens in a chapel-of-ease, these (unless appointed in accordance with one or other of the statutory provisions mentioned below) do not as such have any legal status, nor can they act as *church*wardens unless the churchwardens of the parish give them the authority to do so; and even in that case they act only as the agents of the churchwardens. It is desirable, therefore, that such wardens should be appointed as sidesmen of the parish church, by which means they may be given a legal status as officers of the parish, with the duty of assisting the churchwardens in the exercise of their office.

Under rule 18 of the Church Representation Rules,[1] a procedure is laid down which, if it is followed, enables a 'district church council' to be constituted, and 'deputy churchwardens' to be elected or chosen, for any church or place of worship situated within a parish. And under the Pastoral Measure 1983,[2] in the case of a team ministry established by a pastoral scheme, provision can be made for the election (similar to that contemplated by rule 18 of the Church Representation Rules) of a 'district church council' and 'deputy churchwardens' for any district in the parish which contains a church or place of worship. There is power to delegate particular functions to the deputy churchwardens under both rule 18 and the Measure.

Reference may also here be made to the case of a parish which by virtue of a pastoral scheme has two or more parish churches, each

---

1 See p. 117 for the text of this provision.
2 See p. 151 for the text of this provision.

with its set of two churchwardens. Such churchwardens are by law churchwardens of the whole parish but they may, if they think fit, arrange to perform separate duties in relation to the several parish churches.[1]

It may be mentioned in passing that if the 'wardens' of a chapel-of-ease undertake the care of the funds of the congregation, or of moneys raised by the congregation for a particular purpose such as the maintenance of the fabric, they thereby constitute themselves trustees of the funds or moneys in question, and will be answerable for their proper expenditure. But they are not personally liable on a contract unless they bind themselves expressly.

POWERS AND DUTIES

As to church, churchyard and contents of church

The incumbent is the person in whom the freehold of church and churchyard is normally vested. But possession of both is vested in the incumbent and churchwardens jointly. The main practical consequence of the churchwardens' right to possession is that if any person claims to enter a church for a purpose other than attending a service (or some entry specifically authorized by law) the incumbent and churchwardens together have the right to prevent such entry. This right extends to obtaining an injunction in the civil courts. During a vacancy the churchwardens alone may exercise this right; but any civil proceedings should be commenced in the names of both of them.

While the incumbent has the custody of the key of the church, the churchwardens have the right of access to the church for the proper discharge of their duties.

All the movable furniture and ornaments of the church are in the legal ownership of the churchwardens, but the clergy must be allowed any use of these objects which is necessary for their ministrations. The churchwardens must not remove furnishings or ornaments or introduce new ones without a faculty[2] unless such action amounts merely to replacing any article which is worn out, and even this should only be done in consultation with the incumbent. If any article is stolen, the churchwardens may take all the steps necessary for its recovery and for the prosecution of the thief.

---

1   See p. 64.
2   See Chapter 3.

The care, maintenance, preservation and insurance of the fabric of the church, and of the goods and ornaments thereof, and the repair of the churchyard fence and other structures, are, under the modern law, the responsibility of the parochial church council and not of the churchwardens as such. The Care of Churches and Ecclesiastical Jurisdiction Measure 1991 does, however, impose upon churchwardens the duty to record information about the church, its contents and the land appertaining to it. The churchwardens are also required under the Measure to inspect the fabric of the church annually and to present a report of their findings to the parochial church council. These important provisions are here set out in full.

Care of Churches and Ecclesiastical Jurisdiction Measure 1991 (so far as relating to the duties of churchwardens)

Duties of churchwardens as to recording of information about churches

4. (1) In every parish it shall be the duty of the church-wardens –

    (a) to compile and maintain –

        (i) a full terrier of all lands appertaining to the church;

        (ii) a full inventory of all articles appertaining to the church;

    (b) to insert in a log-book maintained for the purpose a full note of all alterations, additions and repairs to, and other events affecting, the church and the lands and articles appertaining thereto and of the location of any other documents relating to such alterations, additions, repairs and events which are not kept with the log-book.

(2) In carrying out their duty under subsection (1) above the churchwardens shall act in consultation with the minister.

(3) The form of the terrier, inventory and log-book shall accord with such recommendations as the Council for the Care of Churches may make.

(4) The churchwardens shall send a copy of the inventory to such person as the bishop of the diocese concerned may designate from time to time for the purpose of this subsection as soon as practicable after it is compiled and shall notify that person of any alterations at such intervals as the bishop may direct from time to time.

(5)   This section applies in relation to each church in a parish containing more than one church.

Duties of churchwardens as to fabric etc. of churches

5. (1)   In every parish it shall be the duty of the churchwardens –

(a)   at least once in every year, to inspect or cause an inspection to be made of the fabric of the church and all articles appertaining to the church;

(b)   in every year, to deliver to the parochial church council and on behalf of that council to the annual parochial church meeting a report (referred to below as 'the annual fabric report') on the fabric of the church and all articles appertaining to the church, having regard to the inspection or inspections carried out under paragraph (a) above, including an account of all actions taken or proposed during the previous year for their protection and maintenance and, in particular, for the implementation of any recommendation contained in a report under a scheme made in pursuance of section 1 of the Inspection of Churches Measure 1955.[1]

(2)   In carrying out their duty under subsection (1) above the churchwardens shall act in consultation with the minister.

(3)   The annual fabric report shall be delivered to the parochial church council at its meeting next before the annual parochial church meeting and with such amendments as that council may make, to the ensuing annual parochial church meeting.

(4)   The churchwardens shall, as soon as practicable after the beginning of each year, produce to the parochial church council the terrier, the inventory and the log-book relating to events occurring in the previous year and such other records as they consider likely to assist the council in discharging its functions in relation to the fabric of the church and articles appertaining to the church.

(5)   Any terrier, inventory or log-book produced to the parochial church council in accordance with subsection (4) above shall be accompanied by a statement, signed by the churchwardens, to the effect that the contents thereof are accurate.

1   See pp. 87–8.

(6)   This section applies in relation to each church in a parish containing more than one church.

(7)   In this section 'year' means calendar year.

Maintenance of order

It is the duty of churchwardens under Canon F15 to maintain order in the church and churchyard, especially during divine service. They may remove (without using unnecessary force) persons who disturb the performance of the service, or who show that they intend to do so. Whenever possible, the assistance of a police officer should be enlisted to deal with any deliberate disturbance, since a constable's legal powers are more extensive than those of a church-warden. More innocent interference with worship, for instance from young children, is sometimes difficult to control. It may be better to remonstrate with the parent or other accompanying adult than to deal directly with the noisy child. Except in extreme cases, friendly advice given after a service is preferable to immediate, and perhaps misconstrued, intervention.

It is a criminal offence at common law to strike any person in a church or churchyard. And, under the Ecclesiastical Courts Juris-diction Act 1860, riotous, violent, or indecent behaviour in any church, churchyard or burial ground is an offence punishable by fine or imprisonment; so also is the disturbance of a duly authorized preacher, or of any of the clergy celebrating any sacrament or divine service. Any person offending under this Act may be arrested by any constable or churchwarden of the parish or place.

These provisions apply to clergy and laity alike. It is to be observed, however, that the churchwardens cannot interfere with the conduct of the services by the minister unless his or her behav-iour comes within the purview of the Act. In any other case they have no remedy except by way of complaint to the bishop.

Allocation of seats

Churchwardens are entrusted with the duty of providing seats for the parishioners. In this capacity they act as the officers of the bishop, who at common law had the right of disposal of the seats. Their rights and duties in this respect may be limited by some over-riding right of a private person, e.g. when a particular pew is attached to an estate by prescription.[1] Subject, however, to any such rights as these, and

---

1   Or faculty.

subject also, in a church where there are pew-rents, to the rights of the pew-holders, the churchwardens may direct persons where to sit, and where not to sit, and may do this beforehand or for a particular service or for an indefinite period. But they cannot legally give the right to a particular seat for all time, because to do so would divest themselves or their successors of the liberty to rearrange the seating accommodation at a future time. Seats can legally be assigned only to parishioners, and before dispossessing a parishioner of a seat normally occupied by him the churchwardens would be well advised to give him notice of their intention, in order that he may show cause why he should not be so dispossessed.

This control of the seating accommodation belongs to the churchwardens in the interests of good order. They cannot exclude an orderly person on the ground that the church is full if he can stand in such a part of the church as will not interfere with the conduct of the service. It is illegal to demand payment, by way of rent or otherwise, for the exclusive use of a seat, unless there is express statutory permission applicable to the church in question. If a parishioner intrudes himself into a seat contrary to the directions of the churchwardens, they may remove him, provided that they do not use unnecessary force or cause a scandal by disturbing the worship of the church.

Alms and collections

Formerly the minister and churchwardens were entrusted with the disposal, for pious and charitable uses, of alms given at the Communion Service. The rubric in the Book of Common Prayer conferring this authority upon them has, however, been overruled by Canon B17A. As a result Communion alms are now to be treated in the same way as other collections. The power of allocating all collections now rests, under section 7 of the Parochial Church Councils (Powers) Measure 1956, with the incumbent and the parochial church council; the churchwardens as such are not concerned.

Presumably the churchwardens' duties with respect to collections are confined to receiving the money, and holding it (until handed over to the treasurer or other authorized person) as agents for the incumbent and the council.

Vacancy of benefice

Immediately a benefice becomes vacant from any cause other than the resignation of the incumbent, the churchwardens should notify the bishop and the patron. Upon the occurrence of any vacancy, the bishop will probably cause a sequestration warrant to be issued, whereby sequestrators, including the churchwardens, will be appointed. The effect of sequestration is briefly described in Chapter 5.

Under the Parochial Registers and Records Measure 1978, section 6, the custody of the register books of the church rests with the churchwardens during a vacancy in the benefice, except that, where the right of presentation to the benefice is in suspense, and a priest-in-charge has been appointed, the priest-in-charge has the custody of them.

Churchwardens as bishops' officers

The churchwardens are the officers of the bishop, and it is their duty, on the bishop's or archdeacon's visitation at the end of their year of office, to answer such questions as may be put to them about the state of the parish and to report whatever may be amiss. They should also at any other time report to the bishop any irregularity or failure of duty of which he ought to be informed.

ACTIONS BY AND AGAINST CHURCHWARDENS

Apart from any special statutory enactments, churchwardens are not a 'corporation' in the legal sense of having a corporate and continuous existence regardless of changes in the identity of the individual holders of the office; but they have certain attributes of a corporation. Thus they may hold church property, other than land, in perpetual succession; and in the City of London, they may hold land to the same purpose. In relation to any property so held, they can bring an action in their own names in respect of a matter which arose during the period of office of their predecessors, but they cannot be sued in respect of such a matter. Both churchwardens must concur in and be parties to the taking of legal proceedings.

Under modern law, contracts in relation to such matters as the supply of articles for use in the church, or repairs and additions to the fabric and other church property, are properly entered into, not by the churchwardens, but by the parochial church council. The council, therefore, is the proper body to sue or be sued on any such contracts.

9 Other Lay Officers

PARISH CLERK AND SEXTON

By section 7 (iii) of the Parochial Church Council (Powers) Measure 1956, the power to appoint and dismiss the parish clerk and sexton, or any person performing or assisting to perform the duties of parish clerk or sexton, and to determine their salaries and the conditions of the tenure of their offices or of their employment, is vested jointly in the parochial church council and the incumbent.

ORGANIST

Under Canon B20 (as amended) an organist or choirmaster is appointed by the incumbent, with the agreement of the parochial church council. It is usually desirable that the terms of the appointment should be embodied in a written agreement. Termination of the appointment of an organist or choirmaster is likewise to be effected by the incumbent with the agreement of the council; but in exceptional circumstances the archdeacon (or, in the case of the archdeacon's own benefice, the bishop) may dispense with the need to obtain the council's agreement. The office of organist is not known to the common law and an organist as such has no legal status.

The organist, when appointed, is under the control of the incumbent, who is responsible for the music in church as part of the service, and may give directions as to the playing of the organ in the same way as he may with regard to the singing. But the incumbent is enjoined, by Canon B20, to pay due heed to the organist's advice and assistance in the choice of chants, hymns, anthems and other settings and generally in the ordering of the music of the church.

THE VERGER

The strict meaning of the title of verger is the official who carries a 'verge' or mace before a dignitary. In common usage the term denotes the official who takes care of the interior of the fabric of a church. He is the servant of the persons employing him, who should be the parochial church council. It is desirable that there should be a written contract containing the terms of the employment and the conditions on which it may be terminated by either side. The liability in case of an accident to the verger arising out of, or in the course of, his employment should be covered by insurance.

SIDESMEN (OR CHURCHWARDENS' ASSISTANTS)

The annual parochial church meeting of a parish may (but is not obliged to) elect any number of sidesmen or churchwardens' assistants for the forthcoming year. The only qualification for a sidesman is inclusion in the electoral roll of the parish. The duty of sidesmen, as stated in Canon E2, is to promote the cause of true religion in the parish and to assist the churchwardens in the discharge of their duties in maintaining order and decency in the church and churchyard, and especially during the time of divine service.

The practice of 'admitting' their assistants at the same time as the churchwardens themselves are admitted at the annual visitation has tended in recent years to fall into disuse, but is still observed in some places.

CHURCH ARCHITECT OR SURVEYOR

Although not traditionally viewed as one of the lay officers of a parish church, its architectural adviser has important functions which may conveniently be mentioned here.

The Inspection of Churches Measure 1955 requires qualified[1] persons approved by the Advisory Committee[2] to inspect and

---

1 A qualified person has for this purpose to be registered under the Architects Registration Acts 1931 to 1969, or to be a chartered building surveyor.
2 See p. 16.

prepare reports upon churches within the diocese. Such inspections have to be carried out at least once in every five years, hence they are commonly described as quinquennial inspections. The scope of an inspection extends to movables within the church which the archdeacon considers to be of outstanding aesthetic importance or of monetary value.

A copy of the report prepared by the architect or other qualified person has to be submitted to the parochial church council and the archdeacon.

The adviser chosen by the parochial church council from the panel approved by the Advisory Committee normally deals with all architectural matters affecting the church. He or she ought in particular to be consulted beforehand in relation to any proposals of substance which are expected to lead to a faculty application. When a faculty is granted, a condition is commonly attached to it that the authorized works are to be carried out under the supervision of the church architect.

READERS

Readers (often called 'lay readers') are lay officers of the Church whose functions include general pastoral and educational work, and in particular, as regards divine service, officiating at Morning and Evening Prayer (omitting the absolution), the publication of banns of marriage, the reading of the lessons, preaching and distributing the holy sacraments of the Lord's Supper to the people (see Canon E4).

The bishop may, under paragraph 2A of Canon E4, also authorize a reader to conduct burial services with the goodwill of the persons responsible and at the invitation of the minister of the parish or extra-parochial place (such as the chapel of a public institution) where the particular service is to be held.

The use made by the Church of readers has considerably increased in recent years. They usually give their services voluntarily, but it is possible for a reader to be employed in a parish at a stipend.

Any person of either sex who is baptized and confirmed, and a regular communicant of the Church of England, is qualified to become a reader: but a candidate for the office must first undergo an examination of his or her knowledge and competence. A new reader, before being admitted to office, makes a declaration of assent, and that he or she will give due obedience to the bishop; the reader is then admitted by the bishop delivering to him or her the New Testament.

An admitted reader may not exercise office in any diocese (except temporarily, with the bishop's written permission) unless licensed to do so by the bishop of that diocese. Such licence may be revoked by the bishop at any time.

There is a right of appeal to the archbishop against the revocation of a licence.

A register of admitted and licensed readers is kept in each diocese.

DEACONESSES

The order of deaconesses was introduced as an order of women with functions of leading public worship and pastoral care and instruction. It is not one of the 'holy orders' of the Church, and deaconesses are members of the laity for all purposes.[1] They are normally employed in parochial work on a stipendiary basis. With the bishop's permission, and at the incumbent's invitation, a deaconess may say or sing Morning and Evening Prayer (save for the absolution), distribute the sacrament at the Holy Communion, and read the Epistle and Gospel. With the like permission and at the like invitation, she is also enabled (a) to preach at divine service; (b) to church women and, in the absence of the minister, to baptize; (c) with the goodwill of the persons responsible, to officiate at funerals; and (d) to publish banns of marriage at Morning or Evening Prayer.

A deaconess may not exercise her office in any diocese (except temporarily with the bishop's written permission) unless she has been licensed to do so by the bishop of that diocese.

A register of admitted and licensed deaconesses is kept in each diocese.

---

1 Under the Deacons (Ordination of Women) Measure 1986 it is now lawful for a woman to be ordained to the office of deacon and thus to be in holy orders. The status of the order of deaconesses remains unaffected by this Measure; but as no woman is to be admitted as deaconess unless she was accepted for training before February 1987, the order is now effectively closed and women wishing to exercise a comparable ministry will become deacons under the 1986 Measure.

LAY WORKERS

Persons of either sex who have been admitted by the bishop as lay workers are employed in some parishes on a stipendiary basis. Before admitting a lay worker, the bishop must be satisfied that the candidate is baptized, confirmed, and a regular communicant, as well as having had the proper training and possessing the other necessary qualifications. A person who has been admitted to the office of Church Army evangelist is thereby admitted to be a lay worker.

An admitted lay worker may not serve as such in any diocese (except temporarily, with the bishop's written permission) unless licensed to do so by the bishop of that diocese. Before being admitted or licensed the lay worker must make a declaration of assent, and of due obedience to the bishop.

The functions of lay workers include (under the direction of the minister) the leading of public prayer, pastoral care, evangelization, and instruction. With the bishop's permission and at the incumbent's invitation, a lay worker may say or sing Morning and Evening Prayer (save for the absolution), distribute the sacrament at the Holy Communion, and read the Epistle and Gospel. With the like permission and at the like invitation, the lay worker is also enabled (a) to preach at divine service; (b) to church women; (c) with the goodwill of the persons responsible, to officiate at funerals; and (d) to publish banns of marriage.

A register of admitted and licensed lay workers is kept in every diocese.

10 Parochial Church Meetings and Councils

INTRODUCTION

Previously to the Church of England Assembly (Powers) Act 1919,[1] the administration and finances of a parish were, in law, almost exclusively the prerogative of the incumbent and churchwardens. The general body of parishioners had little or no say in these matters, except in so far as they took part in the annual appointment of churchwardens. It is true that parochial church councils had been set up in most urban parishes, but they existed at the will of the incumbent and had no powers except such as he might delegate to them. Their existence was, however, some evidence both of the wishes of the laity to take a larger share of the burdens of parochial administration, and of the desire of the clergy to allow to the laity as a whole a voice in the affairs of the parish.

Parochial church councils were given a legal status for the first time by the Act of 1919, and by the Parochial Church Councils (Powers) Measure 1921, which was one of the first measures to be passed under the powers conferred by the Act. Rules as to the composition of parochial church councils, and as to the procedure in relation to meetings, were set out in a Schedule to the 'Constitution' of the Church Assembly appended to the Act, whilst the Measure defined the functions and powers of such councils.

At the present time, the composition and procedure of parochial church councils are regulated by the Church Representation Rules which constitute Schedule 3 (as since amended) to the Synodical Government Measure 1969, whilst their function and powers are contained in the Parochial Church Councils (Powers) Measure 1956, as amended by the Measure of 1969. The whole of the Parochial Church Councils (Powers) Measure 1956 (as amended)

---

1   See p. 5.

appears in Chapter 11. In addition to the functions conferred by the Measure of 1956, parochial church councils also have a number of particular functions conferred by various other provisions, some of which are mentioned in Chapter 11.

The text of such parts of the Church Representation Rules as are relevant to parochial church councils are set out in the pages which follow. But first, it may be of assistance to state briefly their general effect and the extent of the powers given to the laity in a parish.

The basis of the scheme is the electoral roll. This is a roll of persons who are qualified electors in a parish. They are lay persons of sixteen years of age or upwards, who are baptized and are members of the Church of England or of a Church in communion with the Church of England.[1] They must also sign the form of application set out in an appendix to the Church Representation Rules. A person cannot be a qualified elector unless he or she resides in the parish, or is entered on the electoral roll as a non-resident elector. It is possible, however, for a person to be a qualified elector in any number of parishes at the same time, provided he or she satisfies the necessary conditions as regards each of them.

A non-resident elector, in addition to the qualifications other than residence required of electors who are resident in the parish, must for six months preceding the date of enrolment have habitually attended public worship in the parish on whose roll an entry is sought.

There is provision in the Rules for an annual revision of the electoral roll; also for the preparation of an entirely new roll in the year 2007, and thereafter in every succeeding sixth year.

The Rules provide for the holding, not later than 30th April in each year, of an 'annual parochial church meeting' in which all those whose names are on the electoral roll of the parish are entitled to take part. This meeting elects lay members of the parochial church council; persons so elected must themselves be on the electoral roll of the parish and, as additional qualifications they are required to be actual communicants and at least sixteen years old. Other business which may be conducted at the same meeting consists of (i) the election (triennially) of lay representatives to the

---

1   There is special provision for members of other Churches which subscribe to the doctrine of the Holy Trinity. See p. 96.

deanery synod, (ii) the election of sidesmen, (iii) the receiving of parochial and other reports, and (iv) the general discussion of church and parochial affairs. It is usual for this meeting to be held on the same day as and immediately after the 'meeting of the parishioners' for the appointment of churchwardens.

The incumbent or priest-in-charge is an *ex-officio* member and the *ex-officio* chairman of the parochial church council, which may also include other *ex-officio* members, and co-opted members, in addition to the elected members. The council is a body corporate with perpetual succession. It therefore has a legal existence apart from the members who compose it.

With respect to team and group ministries established by pastoral schemes, and with respect also to new parishes created by pastoral schemes, and to cases where there are two or more parishes within the area of a single benefice or where two or more benefices are held in plurality, the Pastoral Measure 1983 contains special provisions relating to the parochial church meetings and councils of the parishes concerned. The text of these provisions is set out later in this chapter.

THE CHURCH REPRESENTATION RULES (SO FAR AS RELATING TO PAROCHIAL CHURCH MEETINGS AND COUNCILS) WITH NOTES[1]

Table of contents

Part I Church electoral roll

---

1   The Church Representation Rules in their original form were contained in Schedule 3 to the Synodical Government Measure 1969, but the Measure conferred a power to amend the Rules by resolution of the General Synod (a two-thirds majority being required in each House). The Rules were in fact so amended in 1973, 1980, 1981, 1984, 1989, 1994, 1995 and 1999. Amendments were also made by various Measures. They relate not only to representation at the parish level but also to deanery and diocesan synods and the General Synod. The text (as amended) is here reproduced only of those rules which are relevant to representation at the parish level.

Appendix 1

Synodical government forms

Appendix 2

General provisions relating to parochial church councils

Part I

CHURCH ELECTORAL ROLL

Formation of roll

1. (1) There shall be a church electoral roll (in these rules referred to as 'the roll') in every parish, on which the names of lay persons shall be entered as hereinafter provided. The roll shall be available for inspection by bona fide inquirers.

(2) A lay person shall be entitled to have his name entered on the roll of a parish if he[1] is baptized, of sixteen years or

---

1 Under the Interpretation Act 1978, words in the Rules importing the masculine gender include the feminine.

upwards, has signed an application form for enrolment set out in Appendix 1 of these rules and declares himself either –

(a) to be a member of the Church of England or of a Church in communion therewith resident in the parish; or

(b) to be such a member and, not being resident in the parish, to have habitually attended public worship in the parish during a period of six months prior to enrolment; or

(c) to be a member in good standing of a Church which subscribes to the doctrine of the Holy Trinity (not being a Church in communion with the Church of England) and also prepared to declare himself to be a member of the Church of England having habitually attended public worship in the parish during a period of six months prior to enrolment.[1]

Provided that where a lay person will have his sixteenth birthday after the intended revision of the electoral roll or the preparation of a new roll but on or before the date of the annual parochial church meeting, he may complete a form of application for enrolment and his name shall be enrolled but with effect from the date of his birthday.

(3) Where a person resides in an extra-parochial place he shall be deemed for the purposes of these rules to reside in the parish which it abuts, and if there is any doubt in the matter a determination shall be made by the bishop's council and standing committee.[2]

(4) A person shall be entitled to have his name on the roll of each of any number of parishes if he is entitled by virtue of paragraphs (2) and (3) of this rule to have his name entered on each roll;[3] but a person whose name is entered

---

1 This provision has been extensively redrafted. In particular a member of any Church adhering to the doctrine of the Holy Trinity becomes eligible for inclusion.

2 This provision will have to be invoked only on rare occasions.

3 It is legally possible for a person to be 'resident' in two or more places at once, e.g. if he has a house in each place and regularly lives in each house for a substantial part of the year. Thus the qualification of being 'resident' may be satisfied simultaneously as regards each of the parishes in question.

on the roll of each of two or more parishes must choose one of those parishes for the purpose of the provisions of these rules which prescribe the qualifications for election to a deanery synod, a diocesan synod or the General Synod or for membership of a parochial church council under rule 14(1)(f) or of a deanery synod under rule 24(6)(b).[1]

(5) The roll shall, until a parochial church council has been constituted in a parish, be formed and revised by the minister and churchwardens (if any), and shall, after such council has been constituted, be kept and revised by or under the direction of the council. Reference in this rule to a parochial church council shall, so far as may be necessary for giving effect to these rules, be construed as including references to the minister and churchwardens (if any).

(6) Where a new parish is created by a pastoral scheme, the roll of that parish shall in the first instance consist –

(a) in the case of a parish created by the union of two or more former parishes, of the rolls of those parishes combined to form one roll;

(b) in any other case, of the names of the persons whose names are at the date of the coming into existence of the new parish entered on the roll of a parish the whole or any part of which forms part of the new parish and who are either resident in the

---

1 For the text of rule 14(1)(f) see p. 113. Under rule 24(6)(b) (not set out *vebatim* in this book) a person who is on the roll of any parish in a particular deanery, and who is a lay member of the General Synod, or of the diocesan synod of the diocese to which the deanery belongs, is normally an *ex-officio* member of the deanery synod. The object of the latter part of this present rule 1(4) is to prevent any person who is on the rolls of two or more parishes (i) from being on that account eligible for election to the General Synod from more than one diocese (or from more than one electoral area within a diocese), or to any diocesan synod from more than one deanery, or to any deanery synod from more than one parish, or to more than one diocesan or deanery synod; (ii) if he is a member of the General Synod, or of a diocesan or deanery synod from being on that account an *ex-officio* member, under rule 14(1)(e), of more than one parochial church council; and (iii) if he is a member of the General Synod or of a diocesan synod, from being on that account an *ex-officio* member, under rule 24(6)(b), of more than one deanery synod. For all these purposes, he must choose one of the parishes in question.

new parish or have habitually attended public worship therein.[1]

(7) The parochial church council shall appoint a church electoral roll officer to act under its direction for the purpose of carrying out its functions with regard to the electoral roll.[2]

(8) The names of persons who are entitled to have their names entered upon the roll of the parish shall, subject to the provisions of these rules, be from time to time added to the roll. It shall be the duty of the electoral roll officer to keep the roll constantly up to date by the addition and removal of names as from time to time required by these rules, and to report such additions and removals at the next meeting of the parochial church council. When additions and removals have been made by the electoral roll officer a list of such amendments shall be published by being exhibited continuously for not less than fourteen days on or near the principal door of the church or place of worship in the parish to which such amendments relate in such manner as the council may appoint and the list shall contain notification of the right of appeal referred to in rule 43.[3]

(9) Subject to the provisions of this rule, a person's name shall, as the occasion arises, be removed from the roll, if he –

(a) has died; or

(b) becomes a clerk in Holy Orders; or

(c) signifies in writing his desire that his name should be removed; or

(d) ceases to reside in the parish, unless after so ceasing he continues, in any period of six months, habitually to attend public worship in the parish, unless prevented from doing so by illness or other sufficient cause; or

(e) is not resident in the parish and has not habitually attended public worship in the parish during the

---

1 Thus if a new parish is created, any existing electoral roll is to be used as the basis of the electoral roll of the new parish. Where the new parish is formed by the division of an existing parish, only those persons residing or worshipping in the area of the new parish are taken into account. Further names may, of course, be added to the roll in accordance with rule 1(6).

2 Previously to these rules the appointment of an electoral roll officer was not an absolute legal requirement, though in practice many councils did appoint such an officer.

3 See p. 126.

preceding six months, not having been prevented from doing so by illness or other sufficient cause; or

(f) was not entitled to have his name entered on the roll at the time when it was entered.

(10) The removal of a person's name from the roll under any of the provisions of these rules shall be without prejudice to his right to have his name entered again, if he has or acquires that right.

(11) The roll shall where practicable contain a record of the address of every person whose name is entered on the roll, but a failure to comply with this requirement shall not prejudice the validity of any entry on the roll.

Revision of roll and preparation of new roll

2. (1) Except in a year in which a new roll is prepared, the roll of a parish shall be revised annually by or under the direction of the council. Notice of the intended revision in the form[1] set out in section 2 of Appendix 1 to these rules shall be affixed by the minister or under his direction on or near the principal door of every church in the parish and every building in the parish licensed for public worship and remain so affixed for a period of not less than fourteen days before the commencement of the revision. The revision shall be completed not less than fifteen days or more than twenty-eight days before the annual parochial church meeting.

(2) Upon every revision all enrolments or removals from the roll which have been effected since the date of the last revision (or since the formation of the roll, if there has been no previous revision) shall be reviewed, and such further enrolments or removals from the roll as may be required shall be effected.

(3) After the completion of the revision, a copy of the roll as revised shall, together with a list of the names removed from the roll since the last revision (or since the formation of the roll if there has been no previous revision), be published by being exhibited continuously for not less than fourteen days before the annual parochial church meeting on or near the principal door of the parish church in such manner as the council shall appoint. During the period while the copy is so exhibited any errors and omissions in the roll may be cor-

---

1 See p. 139.

rected, but subject thereto and to the provisions of rule 1(2),[1] no names shall be added to or removed from the roll during the period in any year between the completion of the revision and the close of the annual parochial church meeting.

(4)[2] Not less than two months before the annual parochial church meeting in the year 2007 and every succeeding sixth year notice in the form set out in section 3 of Appendix 1 to these rules shall be affixed by the minister or under his direction on or near the principal door of every church in the parish and every building in the parish licensed for public worship and remain so affixed for a period of not less than fourteen days. On the affixing of the notice a new roll shall be prepared.

At every service held on each of the two Sundays within the period of fourteen days beginning with the date of the affixing of the notice or, in the case of a church in which no service is held on either of those Sundays, at every service held in that church on the first Sunday after that date the person conducting the service shall inform the congregation of the preparation of the new roll.

(5) The parochial church council shall take reasonable steps to inform every person whose name is entered on the previous roll that a new roll is being prepared and that if he wishes to have his name entered on the new roll he must apply for enrolment. No such steps need be taken with respect to any person whose name could be removed from the previous roll under rule 1(9).

(6) The new roll shall be prepared by entering upon it the names of persons entitled to entry under rule 1(2), and a

---

1 The name of a person whose sixteenth birthday falls between the revision of the roll and the date of the annual parochial church meeting may therefore be added to the roll during this period.

2 Sub-paragraphs (4) to (7) provide for the preparation of an entirely new electoral roll in every parish in the year 2007, and in every succeeding sixth year. On every such occasion, every person whose name was entered on the previous roll must make a fresh application in order to be entered on the new roll. The requirement of a new roll at intervals of six years was imposed for the first time by these rules. Its object is to procure a periodical re-checking of every single name on the roll, and thus to ensure (as far as possible) the exclusion of all disqualified persons and of all persons who have ceased to take an active interest in Church affairs.

fresh application shall be required from persons whose names were entered on the previous roll. A person whose name was so entered shall not be disqualified for entry on the new roll by reason only of his failure to comply with the conditions specified in rule 1(2)(b) and (c) if he was prevented from doing so by illness or other sufficient cause, and the circumstances shall be stated on the application form. The preparation of the new roll shall be completed not less than fifteen days or more than twenty-eight days before the annual parochial church meeting.

(7) After the completion of the new roll, a copy shall be published by being exhibited continuously for not less than fourteen days before the annual parochial church meeting on or near the principal door of the parish church in such manner as the council shall appoint. During the period while the copy is exhibited any errors and omissions in the roll may be corrected, but subject thereto, and to the provisions of rule 1(2) no names may be added to or removed from the roll during the period in any year between the completion of the new roll and the close of the annual parochial church meeting. On the publication of the new roll it shall come into effect and the previous roll shall cease to have effect.

(8) Upon the alteration of the boundaries of any parishes the parochial church council of the parish from which any area is transferred shall inquire from the persons resident in that area whose names are entered on the roll of the parish, whether they wish to have their names transferred to the roll of the other parish. The parochial church council shall remove the names of persons answering in the affirmative from its own roll and shall inform the parochial church council of the parish in which such persons now reside, which shall enter the names on its roll without any application for enrolment being required.

Procedural provisions relating to entry and removal of names

3. (1) When a person applying for enrolment on the roll of any parish signifies his desire that his name should be removed from the roll of any other parish, notice of that fact shall be sent by the parochial church council receiving the application to the parochial church council of that other parish.

(2)   When the name of any person is removed from the roll of the parish owing to his having become resident in another parish notice of that fact shall, whenever possible, be sent by the parochial church council of the first mentioned parish to the parochial church council of the last mentioned parish.

Certification of numbers on rolls[1]

4.   Not later than 1st June the chairman, vice-chairman, secretary or church electoral roll officer of the parochial church council shall notify in writing the secretary of the diocesan synod of the number of names on the roll of each parish as at the date of the annual meeting and a copy of such notification shall be affixed at or near to the principal door of every church in the parish and every building licensed for public worship in the parish when notification is sent to the secretary of the diocesan synod, and shall remain so affixed for a period of not less than fourteen days.

Provision with respect to person whose name is on guild church roll

5.   (1)   A person whose name is entered on the roll of a guild church shall for the purpose of the provisions of these rules which prescribe the qualifications for election to a deanery synod, a diocesan synod or the House of Laity of the General Synod, or for membership of a deanery synod under rule 24(6)(b), be deemed to be a person whose name is on the roll of the parish in which the guild church is, and references in those provisions or in rule 1(4) to a person whose name is on the roll of a parish or on the roll of each of two or more parishes, and in rule 46 to entry on the roll of a parish, shall be construed accordingly.

(2)   In this rule 'guild church' means a church in the City of

---

1   Rule 4 is necessary because the number of lay representatives elected by a parish to a deanery synod depends on the number of persons on the electoral roll of the parish: and similarly, the number of lay representatives elected by a deanery to a diocesan synod, or by a diocese to the General Synod, depends on the aggregate number of the names on the rolls of all the parishes in the deanery or the diocese (as the case may be). Rules 25(2) and 31(6) and 36, not included in this book, deal with the administration of these arrangements by the diocesan synod.

London designated and established as a guild church under the City of London (Guild Churches) Acts 1952 and 1960.[1]

Part II
PAROCHIAL CHURCH MEETINGS AND COUNCILS
ANNUAL MEETINGS
Annual meetings

6. (1) In every parish there shall be held not later than 30th April in each year[2] the annual parochial church meeting (hereafter in these rules referred to as 'the annual meeting').

(2) All lay persons whose names are entered on the roll of the parish shall be entitled to attend the annual meeting and to take part in its proceedings, and no other lay person shall be so entitled.[3]

(3) A clerk in Holy Orders shall be entitled to attend the annual meeting of a parish and take part in its proceedings –

(a) if he is either beneficed in or licensed to the parish or any other parish in the area of the benefice to which the parish belongs; or

---

1　As to guild churches generally, see pp. 26–7. The object of this rule is to put any person who is on the roll of a guild church in the same position, as regards eligibility for election to or membership of any synod, as if he were on the roll of the parish in which the guild church is situated. For the text of rule 1(4) and the effect of rule 24(6)(b) (not set out *verbatim* in this book) see pp. 96–7. Rule 46 (also not set out *verbatim*) provides generally for the vacation of the seats of synod members who cease to qualify for membership.

2　Previously to these rules, the meeting had to be held 'not later in the year than the week following Easter week'.

3　The rules do not expressly lay down whether members of the general public are entitled to be admitted to the meeting to observe the proceedings and it is thought that the meeting itself can resolve either to admit or to exclude them. Where, as is frequently the arrangement, the meeting immediately follows the meeting of parishioners for the appointment of churchwardens, lay persons who are entitled to attend the meeting of parishioners, but who are not on the electoral roll, should be called upon either (if the public are not being admitted) to leave at the end of the meeting of parishioners, or (if the public are being admitted) to remain, if they so desire, as observers only.

(b) if he is resident in the parish and is not beneficed in or licensed to any other parish;[1] or

(c) if he is not resident in the parish and is not beneficed or licensed to any other parish, the parochial church council with the concurrence of the minister has declared him to be an habitual worshipper in the parish, such declaration being effective until the conclusion of the annual meeting in the year in which a new roll is prepared under rule 2 or his ceasing to be an habitual worshipper in the parish whichever is the earlier, but without prejudice to a renewal of such declaration; or

(d) if he is a co-opted member of the parochial church council in accordance with rule 14 (1)(h).

(4) Without prejudice to paragraphs (2) and (3) of this rule –

(a) all the members of the team of a team ministry shall be entitled to attend, and take part in the proceedings of, the annual meeting of the parish or each of the parishes in the area of the benefice for which the team ministry is established, and where the area of a group ministry includes the area of a benefice for which a team ministry is established, all the vicars in that ministry shall be entitled to attend, and take part in the proceedings of, the annual meeting of each of the other parishes in the area for which the group ministry is established;

(b) all the incumbents and priests-in-charge in a group ministry shall be entitled to attend, and take part in the proceedings of, the annual meeting of each of the parishes in the area for which the group ministry is established.

(5) Where two or more benefices are held in plurality and a team ministry is, or is to be, established for the area of one of those benefices, then, if a pastoral scheme provides for extending the operation of the team ministry, so long as the plurality continues, to the area of any other benefice

---

1   Section 12(4) of the Cathedrals Measure 1999 provides that residentiary canons and other clergy of a parish church cathedral may attend the annual parochial church meeting of the parish of that cathedral, whether or not they are resident in the parish.

so held, paragraph (4) of this rule shall have effect as if the references to the area of the benefice were references to the combined area of the benefices concerned.

Convening of meeting

7. (1) The annual meeting shall be convened by the minister of the parish by a notice in the form set out in section 4 of Appendix 1 to these rules affixed on or near to the principal door of every church in the parish, and every building licensed for public worship in the parish, for a period including the last two Sundays before the day of the meeting.

(2) The annual meeting shall be held at such place on such date and at such hour as shall be directed by the previous annual meeting, or by the parochial church council (which may vary any direction given by a previous annual meeting) or in the absence of any such direction as shall be appointed by the minister.

(3) During the vacancy of the benefice or curacy or when the minister is absent or incapacitated by illness or any other cause, the vice-chairman of the parochial church council, or if there is no vice-chairman, or if he is unable or unwilling to act, the secretary of or some other person appointed by that council shall have all the powers vested in the minister under this rule.

(4) The annual meeting shall be held at a place within the parish unless the parochial church council decide otherwise.

(5) The minister of a new parish created by a pastoral scheme, or, in the absence of the minister, a person appointed by the bishop, shall as soon as possible after the scheme comes into operation convene a special parochial church meeting, and, subject to paragraph (6) of this rule, the provisions of these rules relating to the convening and conduct of the annual meeting shall apply to a special meeting convened under this pararaph.

(6) A special meeting so convened and held in the month of November or the month of December may, if the meeting so resolves, be for all purposes under these rules the annual meeting for the succeeding year, and a special meeting so convened shall in any event be for all such

purposes the annual meeting for the year in which it is so convened and held.

Chairman

8. (1) The minister, if present, or if he is not present, the vice-chairman of the parochial church council, or subject to paragraph (2) of this rule, if he also is not present, a chairman chosen by the annual meeting shall preside thereat.

(2) Where a parish is in the area of a benefice for which a team ministry is established, and a vicar in that ministry is entitled to preside at an annual meeting of that parish by virtue of a provision in a pastoral scheme or the bishop's licence assigning to the vicar the duties, or a share in the duties, of the chairmanship of the annual meeting of that parish, then, if both he and the vice-chairman of the parochial church council are not present at that meeting, but the rector in that ministry is present, the rector shall preside thereat.

(3) In the case of an equal division of votes, the chairman shall have a second or casting vote, unless it is a case where rule 11(8) applies; but no clerical chairman shall have a vote in the election of the parochial representatives of the laity.[1]

Business

9. (1) The annual meeting shall receive from the parochial church council and shall be free to discuss –

(a) a report on changes in the roll since the last annual parochial church meeting or, in a year in which a new roll is prepared, a report on the numbers entered on the new roll;

(b) an annual report on the proceedings of the parochial church council and the activities of the parish generally;

---

1 Previously to these rules, a clerical chairman was permitted a casting vote in an election though not an original vote, but now the casting vote is also disallowed and where there is an equality of votes the decision is by lot; see rule 11(8). That the spin of a coin should be preferred to the wisdom of the presiding cleric may be thought a somewhat extreme application of the principle of excluding all clerical influence in the election of lay representatives.

    (c)   the financial statements of the parochial church council for the year ending on 31st December immediately preceding the meeting, independently examined or audited as provided by paragraph (3) hereof;

    (d)   a report upon the fabric, goods and ornaments of the church or churches of the parish under section 5 of the Care of Churches and Ecclesiastical Jurisdiction Measure 1991;[1] and

    (e)   a report on the proceedings of the deanery synod.

(2)   The council shall cause a copy of the said roll to be available for inspection at the meeting.

(3)   The said financial statements shall –

    (a)   be independently examined or audited in such manner as shall be prescribed in accordance with rule 54(8);[2]

    (b)   be considered and, if thought fit, approved by the parochial church council and signed by the chairman presiding at the meeting of the council; and

    (c)   be displayed for a continuous period of at least seven days before the annual meeting, including at least one Sunday when the church is used for worship, on a notice-board either inside or outside the church.

(4)   The annual report referred to in paragraph (1)(b) above and the said financial statements shall be prepared in such form as shall be prescribed in accordance with rule 54(8)[3] hereof for consideration by the annual meeting. Following such meeting the council shall cause copies of the annual report and statements to be sent within twenty-eight days of the annual meeting to the secretary of the diocesan board of finance for retention by the board.

(5)   The annual meeting shall in the manner provided by rule 11 –

    (a)   elect in every third year parochial representatives of

---

1   See p. 82.
2   See p. 145 footnote 1 for the examination or audit of accounts.
3   Rule 54(8) enables the General Synod to prescribe the form of these documents.

the laity to the deanery synod;

(b) elect parochial representatives of the laity to the parochial church council;

(c) appoint sidesmen;[1]

(d) appoint the independent examiner or auditor to the council for a term of office ending at the close of the next annual meeting, provided that such person shall not be a member of the council;

and the elections and appointments shall be carried out in the above order.

(6) Without prejudice to the foregoing provisions and rule 7(6), a special parochial church meeting convened under rule 7(5) shall, in addition to other business –

(a) decide on the number of members of the parochial church council who are to be elected representatives of the laity;

(b) elect in the manner provided by rule 11 parochial representatives of the laity to the deanery synod, if such representatives are required to be elected in the year for which that meeting is the annual meeting by virtue of rule 7(6).

(7) Any person entitled to attend the annual meeting may ask any question about parochial church matters, or bring about a discussion of any matter of parochial or general church interest, by moving a general resolution or by moving to give any particular recommendation to the council in relation to its duties.

(8) The annual meeting shall have power to adjourn and to determine its own rules of procedure.

(9) The secretary of the parochial church council (or another person appointed by the meeting in his place) shall act as a clerk of the annual meeting, and shall record the minutes thereof.

Qualifications of persons to be chosen or elected by annual meetings

10. (1) Subject to the provisions of rule 1(3), and sub-paragraph (3) of this rule, the qualifications of a person to be elected a parochial representative of the laity to either the parochial church council or the deanery synod are that –

---

1 The election of sidesmen is in fact optional.

(a)   his name is entered on the roll of the parish and, unless he is under the age of 18 years at the date of the election, has been so entered for at least the preceding period of six months;

(b)   he is an actual communicant as defined in rule 54(1);[1] and

(c)   he is of sixteen years or upwards.

(2)   The qualification of a person to be appointed a sidesman is that his name is entered on the roll of the parish.

(3)   No person shall be nominated for election under rule 9 –

(a)   to serve on either the parochial church council, or the deanery synod unless he has signified his consent to serve, or there is in the opinion of the meeting sufficient evidence of his willingness to serve;

(b)   to serve on the parochial church council, if he has been disqualified under rule 46A.[2]

Conduct of elections at annual meetings

11. (1)   Subject to the provisions of any scheme made under rule 12 and for the time being in force, this rule shall apply to all elections at annual meetings.

(2)   All candidates for elections at an annual meeting must be nominated and seconded by persons entitled to attend the annual meeting, and in the case of parochial representatives of the laity, by persons whose names are entered on the roll of the parish. A candidate shall be nominated or seconded either before the meeting in writing or at the meeting.

(3)   If the number of candidates nominated is not greater than the number of seats to be filled, the candidates nominated shall forthwith be declared elected.

(4)   If more candidates are nominated than there are seats to be filled, the election shall take place at the annual meeting.

(5)   No clerk in Holy Orders shall be entitled to vote in the election of any parochial representative of the laity.[3]

(6)   Each person entitled to vote shall have as many votes as there are seats to be filled but may not give more than one vote to any one candidate.

---

1   p. 134.

2   See pp. 129–30.

3   Previously to these rules, a clerical chairman had a casting though not an original vote.

(7) Votes may be given –
   (a) by show of hands; or
   (b) if one or more persons object –
      (i) on voting papers signed by the voter on the reverse thereof; or
      (ii) if at least one-tenth of the persons present and voting at the meeting so request, on numbered voting papers.[1]

(8) (a) Where owing to an equality of votes an election is not decided the decision between the persons for whom the equal numbers of votes have been cast shall be taken by lot.

   (b) When an election or any stage of an election is recounted, either on appeal or at the request of the presiding officer or of a candidate, if the original count and the recount are identical at the point when a lot must be drawn to resolve a tie, the original lot shall be used to make the determination.

(9) The result of any election by an annual meeting shall be announced as soon as practicable by the person presiding over the election, and a notice of the result shall in every case be affixed on or near the principal door of every church in the parish and every building licensed for public worship in the parish, and shall bear the date on which the result is declared. The notice shall remain affixed for not less than fourteen days. Thereafter the secretary of the parochial church council shall hold a list of the names and addresses of the members of the council which shall be available for inspection on reasonable notice being given by any person who either is resident in the parish or has his name on the electoral roll, but the secretary shall not be bound to provide a copy of such list.

(10) Names and addresses of parochial representatives of the laity elected to the deanery synod shall be sent by the secretary of the parochial church council to the diocesan electoral registration officer appointed in accordance

---

1   It seems, however, that the use of voting papers is mandatory when postal votes have been received; see rules 12(2) and (3), pp. 111–12.

with rule 29¹ and to the secretary of the deanery synod.

(11) Where a vote is conducted in accordance with paragraph (7)(b)(ii) above, a record shall be made of the identity of each person to whom a numbered voting paper is issued and any such record, so long as it is retained, shall be kept separate from the voting papers.

Variation of method of election

12. (1) The annual meeting may pass a resolution which provides that the election of parochial representatives of the laity to the parochial church council or to the deanery synod or to both that council and that synod shall be conducted by the method of the single transferable vote under rules, with the necessary modifications, made by the General Synod under rule 39(8) and for the time being in force, except that where the vote is conducted in accordance with Rule 11(7)(b)(ii), these rules shall have effect with the omission of any requirement that the voting paper be signed by the voter.²

(2) The annual meeting may pass a resolution which provides that any person entitled to attend the annual meeting and vote in the elections of parochial representatives of the laity to the parochial church council or to the deanery synod or to both that council and that synod may

---

1 Rule 29 (not set out *verbatim* in this book) provides for the appointment, by the bishop's council and standing committee of the diocesan synod, of a diocesan electoral registration officer responsible for keeping registers of clerical and lay members of deanery synods. The registers are used for the purpose of elections to the diocesan synod.

2 Rule 39(8), not printed *verbatim* in this book, provides for the making of rules by the General Synod for elections by the single transferable vote system, which rules apply to elections to the General Synod itself. In 1980, by the introduction of rule 10A, it was made optional for the annual meeting of any parish to make provision for the election of representatives of the parish to the deanery synod, and of members of the parochial church council, by proportional representation. In 1984 rule 10A, now rule 12, was amended to substitute the method of the single transferable vote for proportional representation. Under this system, each voter indicates in order of preference the candidates whom he supports. When the votes are counted the surplus first preference votes are redistributed in accordance with the second choice on those voting papers. The process is repeated until sufficient candidates each have a majority. While a more representative system, it is not at present much used at parish level because of the complexity of making the count. The Electoral Reform Society now, however, sells a computer program which greatly simplifies the exercise.

make application in the form set out in section 4A of Appendix 1 for a postal vote.

(3) Where applications for postal votes have been received by the date specified in the notice convening the annual meeting and where the number of candidates nominated for an election referred to in paragraph (2) of this rule is greater than the number of seats to be filled, the annual meeting shall appoint a presiding officer who shall not be a candidate in the election. Voting papers shall be distributed to each person present at the meeting entitled to vote and completed papers shall be returned into the custody of the presiding officer before the close of the meeting. The presiding officer shall ensure that persons who have made application for a postal vote shall be sent or have delivered a voting paper within 48 hours of the close of the meeting such paper to be returned to the presiding officer within such period of not less than seven days nor more than fourteen days from the date of the meeting as the presiding officer shall specify.

(4) A resolution passed under this rule shall be invalid unless approved by at least two-thirds of the persons present and voting at the annual meeting nor shall it be operative until the next ensuing annual meeting. Such resolution may be rescinded by a subsequent resolution passed in the same manner.

Conduct of elections of churchwardens
13. (1) Elections of churchwardens under the Churchwardens Measure 2001[1] shall be conducted, announced and notified in the same manner as elections under rule 11, except that all persons entitled to attend the meeting of parishioners other than the minister shall be entitled to nominate and vote at such elections of churchwardens.

(2) . . . (Repealed)

PAROCHIAL CHURCH COUNCIL
Members
14. (1) Subject to the provisions of rule 1(4) and paragraph (3) of this rule, the parochial church council shall consist of –
(a) all clerks in Holy Orders beneficed in or licensed to the parish;

---

1 See p. 64 *et seq.* for the text of this Measure and notes thereto.

(aa)   any clerk in Holy Orders who is duly authorised to act as chairman of meetings of the council by the bishop in accordance with paragraph 5(b) of Appendix II to these rules;[1]

(b)   any deaconess or lay worker licensed to the parish;

(c)   in the case of a parish in the area of a benefice for which a team ministry is established, all the members of the team of that ministry;

(d)   the churchwardens, and any deputy churchwardens who are ex-officio members of the parochial church council by virtue of a scheme made under rule 18(4) of these rules, being actual communicants[2] whose names are on the roll of the parish;

(e)   such, if any, of the readers who are licensed to that parish or licensed to an area which includes that parish and whose names are on the roll of the parish, as the annual meeting may determine;

(f)   all persons whose names are on the roll of the parish and who are lay members of any deanery synod, diocesan synod or the General Synod;

(g)   six representatives of the laity where there are not more than 50 names on the electoral roll, nine such representatives where there are not more than 100 names on the roll and, where there are more than 100 names on the roll, a further three such representatives for every 100 (or part thereof) names on the roll up to a maximum of 15 such members, and so that the aforesaid numbers 'six', 'nine, 'three' and '15' may be altered from time to time by a resolution passed at any annual meeting, but such resolution shall not take effect before the next ensuing annual meeting; and

(h)   co-opted members, if the parochial church council so decides, not exceeding in number one-fifth of the representatives of the laity elected under the last preceding sub-paragraph of this paragraph or two persons whichever shall be the greater, and being

---

1   See p. 147 for the appointment of an ordained person to take the chair, in the absence of an incumbent, at parochial church council meetings.

2   The expression 'actual communicant' extends to a person permitted to receive Holy Communion albeit not a member of the Church of England.

either clerks in Holy Orders or actual lay communicants of sixteen years of age or upwards. The term of office of a co-opted member shall be until the conclusion of the next annual meeting; but without prejudice to his being co-opted on subsequent occasions for a similar term, subject to and in accordance with the provisions of these rules.

(2) Any person chosen, appointed or elected as a churchwarden of a parish, being an actual communicant whose name is on the roll of the parish, shall as from the date on which the choice, appointment or election, as the case may be, is made be a member of the parochial church council of the parish by virtue of this paragraph until he is admitted to the office of churchwarden, and he shall thereafter continue to be a member of that council by virtue of paragraph 1(d) of this rule unless and until he ceases to be qualified for membership by virtue of that sub-paragraph.[1]

(3) A person shall cease to be a member of a parochial church council –

(a) if his name is removed from the roll of the parish under rule 1, on the date on which his name is removed;

(b) if he refuses or fails to apply for enrolment when a new roll is being prepared, on the date on which the new roll is completed;

(c) if he is or becomes disqualified under rule 46A,[2] from the date on which the disqualification takes effect;

but, so far as the provisions of (a) and (b) above are concerned, shall be without prejudice to any right which that council may have to make that person a co-opted member.

(4) Where a group ministry is established the incumbents of all benefices in the group, every priest in charge of any benefice therein and where the area of the group ministry includes the area of a benefice for which a team ministry is established, all the vicars in that ministry shall be

---

1 Under this provision, introduced in 1980, a newly chosen, appointed or elected churchwarden having the necessary qualifications, although he does not take office as churchwarden until admitted as such, will at once become a member of the parochial church council. After having been admitted as churchwarden, unless in the meantime he has become disqualified, he will continue an *ex-officio* member of the council until the admission as churchwarden of his successor in office.

2 See pp. 129–30.

entitled to attend meetings of the parochial church councils of all the parishes in the area for which the group ministry is established. They shall be entitled to receive documents circulated to members of councils of which they are not themselves members and to speak but not to vote at meetings of such councils.

(5) Where two or more benefices are held in plurality and a team ministry is, or is to be, established for the area of one of those benefices, then, if a pastoral scheme provides for extending the operation of the team ministry, so long as the plurality continues, to the area of any other benefice so held, paragraphs (1)(c) and (4) of this rule shall have effect as if the references to the area of the benefice were references to the combined area of the benefices concerned.

General provisions relating to parochial church councils

15. The provisions in Appendix 2 to these rules shall have effect with respect to parochial church councils, and with respect to the officers, the meetings and the proceedings thereof:

Provided that a parochial church council may, with the consent of the diocesan synod, vary the said provisions in their application to the council.

Term of office

16. (1) Subject to the following provisions of these rules, representatives of the laity serving on the parochial church council by virtue of rule 14(1)(g) shall hold office from the conclusion of the annual meeting at which they were elected until the conclusion of the third annual meeting thereafter, one third retiring and being elected each year, but, subject to rule 17, shall on retirement be eligible for re-election.[1]

(2) Where a representative of the laity resigns or otherwise fails to serve for his full term of office the casual vacancy shall be filled for the remainder of his term of office in accordance with rule 48(1).

(3) Notwithstanding the preceding provisions of this rule an annual meeting may decide that the representatives of the laity serving by virtue of rule 14(1)(g) shall retire from

---

1 The general effect of rule 16 is to give annual meetings the choice between electing one-third of the lay membership each year (thus giving members a three-year term of office) and holding an election for all lay members every year. The methods of changing from one system to the other are as set out in rule 16(3) and 16(6).

office at the conclusion of the annual meeting next following their election, but any such decision shall not affect the terms of office as members of the parochial church council of those due to retire from office at the conclusion of an annual meeting held after that at which the decision was taken.

(4) A decision taken under paragraph (3) above shall be reviewed by the annual meeting at least once every six years; and on any such review the annual meeting may revoke the decision, in which case paragraph (1) above shall apply unless and until a further decision is taken under paragraph (3).

(5) Persons who are members of a parochial church council by virtue of their election as lay members of a deanery synod shall hold office as members of the council for a term beginning with the date of their election and ending with the 31st May next following the election of their successors.[1]

(6) At an annual meeting at which all the representatives of the laity serving by virtue of rule 14(1)(g) are elected to hold office in accordance with paragraph (1) above, lots shall be drawn to decide which third of the representatives is to retire in the first year following that in which the meeting is held, which third is to retire in the second year and which third is to retire in the third year.

Limitation on years of service

17. The annual meeting may decide that no representative of the laity being a member of the parochial church council by virtue of rule 14 (1)(g)[2] may hold office after the date of that meeting for more than a specified number of years continuously and may also decide that after a specified interval a person who has ceased to be eligible by reason of such decision may again stand for election as representative of the laity on the council.

---

1   The reason for this rule is that an elected member of the deanery synod continues to be a member thereof down to and including 31st May in the year in which new elections are held, and it is deemed expedient that so long as he is such a member, he should remain on the parochial church council. It should, however, be noted that if, at the relevant annual meeting, a sitting member of the deanery synod is not re-elected to that synod, the fact that his *ex-officio* membership of the parochial church council is prolonged till the ensuing 31st May is no bar to his election as an ordinary member of the council, for the normal term, at the same annual meeting.

2   See p. 113. This limitation may only apply to elected lay representatives.

Parishes with more than one place of worship

18. (1)   In any parish where there are two or more churches or places of worship the annual meeting may make a scheme which makes provision for either or both of the following purposes, that is to say –

(a)   for the election of the representatives of the laity to the parochial church council in such manner as to ensure due representation of the congregation of each church or place; and

(b)   for the election by the annual meeting for any district in the parish in which a church or place of worship is situated of a district church council for that district.

(2)   A scheme for the election of any district church council or councils under the preceding paragraph shall provide for the election of representatives of the laity on to such council, for *ex-officio* members and for the chairmanship of such council and shall contain such other provisions as to membership and procedure as shall be considered appropriate by the annual meeting.

(3)   Such a scheme may also provide for the delegation by the parochial church council to a district church council of such functions as may be specified in the scheme and, subject to the provisions of the scheme, the parochial church council may by resolution also delegate to a district church council such of its functions as it shall think fit but not including (in either case) the functions of the parochial church council –

(i)   in respect of producing the financial statement of the parish;

(ii)   as an interested party under Part I of the Pastoral Measure 1983;

(iii)   under Part II of the Patronage (Benefices) Measure 1986;[1]

(iv)   under section 3 of the Priests (Ordination of Women) Measure 1993.[2]

(4)   A scheme may provide for the election or choice of one or two deputy churchwardens, and for the delegation to him or them of such functions of the churchwardens relating to any church or place as the scheme may specify, and the churchwardens may, subject to the

---

1   See p. 55.
2   See p. 47

scheme, delegate such of their said functions as they think fit to the deputy churchwarden or churchwardens. The scheme may also provide for the deputy churchwardens to be *ex-officio* members of the parochial church council.

(5) No scheme under this rule shall be valid unless approved by at least two-thirds of the persons present and voting at the annual meeting nor shall the scheme provide for it to come into operation until such date as the bishop's council and standing committee may determine being a date not later than the next ensuing annual meeting. Every such scheme shall on its approval be communicated to the bishop's council and standing committee of the diocesan synod which may determine –

(a)   that the scheme shall come into operation; or

(b)   that the scheme shall not come into operation; or

(c)   that the scheme shall come into operation with specified amendments, if such amendments are approved by an annual or special parochial church meeting and the scheme as amended is approved by at least two-thirds of the persons present and voting at that meeting.

(6) A special parochial church meeting of a parish to which this rule applies may be convened for the purpose of deciding whether to make such a scheme, and where such a meeting is convened the foregoing provisions shall have effect with the substitution for references to the annual meeting of references to the special meeting.

(7) Where a pastoral scheme establishing a team ministry, or an instrument of the bishop made by virtue of that scheme[1] makes, in relation to a parish in the area of the benefice for which the team ministry is established, any provision which may be made by a scheme under this rule, no scheme under this rule relating to that parish shall provide for the scheme to come into operation until on or after the date on which the provisions in question of

---

1   See Schedule 3, paragraph 4 of the Pastoral Measure 1983 printed on p. 151 and p. 153 footnote 1.

the pastoral scheme or of the instrument, as the case may be, cease to have effect.

(8) A scheme under this rule may be amended by a subsequent scheme passed in accordance with the provisions of paragraph (4) of this rule.

(9) Every member of the team of a team ministry shall have a right to attend the meetings of any district church council elected for any district in a parish in the area of the benefice for which the team ministry is established.

(10) This rule shall be without prejudice to the appointment, in parishes with more than one parish church, of two churchwardens for each church under section 27(5) of the Pastoral Measure 1983.[1]

(11) In this rule 'place of worship' means a building or part of a building licensed for public worship.

Joint parochial church councils

19. (1) Where there are two or more parishes within the area of a single benefice or two or more benefices are held in plurality, the annual meetings of all or some of the parishes in the benefice or benefices may make a joint scheme to provide –

(a) for establishing a joint parochial church council (hereinafter referred to as 'the joint council') comprising the ministers of the parishes and such numbers of representatives of each of those parishes elected by and from among the other members of the parochial church council of the parish as may be specified in the scheme;

(b) for the chairmanship, meetings and procedure of the joint council;

(c) subject to paragraph 20 of Schedule 2 to the Patronage (Benefices) Measure 1986 for the delegation by the parochial church council of each such parish to the joint council of such of its functions,

---

1   Section 27 (5) of the Pastoral Measure 1983 has in part been replaced by section 1(2) of the Churchwardens Measure 2001. Under both Measures, where a parish has more than one parish church, two churchwardens shall be appointed for each church. All churchwardens are, however, to be churchwardens of the whole parish except so far as they arrange to perform separate duties in relation to the several parish churches.

other than its functions as an interested party[1] under Part I of the Pastoral Measure 1983 and its functions under section 3 of the Priests (Ordination of Women) Measure 1993, as may be so specified.

(2) Subject to the scheme and to any pastoral scheme or order made under paragraph 13 of Schedule 3 to the said Measure and to paragraph 20 of Schedule 2 to the Patronage (Benefices) Measure 1986, the parochial church council of any such parish may delegate to the joint council such of its functions, other than its functions as an interested party under the said Part I and its functions under section 3 of the Priests (Ordination of Women) Measure 1993,[2] as it thinks fit.

(3) The joint council shall meet from time to time for the purpose of consulting together on matters of common concern.

(4) No scheme under this rule shall be valid unless approved by at least two-thirds of the persons present and voting at the annual meeting nor shall the scheme provide for it to come into operation until such date as the bishop's council and standing committee may determine being a date not later than the next ensuing annual meeting. Every such scheme shall on its approval be communicated to the bishop's council which may determine –

(a) that the scheme shall come into operation; or

(b) that the scheme shall not come into operation; or

(c) that the scheme shall come into operation with specified amendments, if such amendments are approved by an annual or special parochial church meeting and the scheme as amended is approved by at least two-thirds of the persons present and voting at that meeting.

(5) A special parochial church meeting of a parish to which this rule applies may be convened for the purpose of deciding whether to join in making such a scheme, and where such a meeting is convened the foregoing provisions shall have effect with the substitution for references to the annual meeting of references to the special meeting.

---

1 See p. 21 for the position of interested parties.
2 See p. 47.

(6) Where a pastoral scheme or order, or any instrument of the bishop made by virtue of such a scheme or order,[1] establishes a joint parochial church council for two or more of the parishes in a single benefice or two or more of the parishes in benefices held in plurality, no scheme under this rule relating to those parishes shall provide for the scheme to come into operation until on or after the date on which the provisions of the pastoral scheme, pastoral order or instrument, as the case may be, establishing the joint parochial church council cease to have effect.

(7) Where provisions of a pastoral scheme or order for the holding of benefices in plurality are terminated under section 18(2) of the Pastoral Measure 1983 any provision of a scheme under this rule establishing a joint parochial church council for all or some of the parishes of those benefices and the other provisions thereof affecting that council shall cease to have effect on the date on which the first mentioned provisions cease to have effect.

(8) A scheme under this rule may be amended or revoked by a subsequent scheme passed in accordance with the provisions of paragraph (4) of this rule.

Team councils

20. (1) Where a team ministry is established for the area of a benefice which comprises more than one parish the annual meetings of the parishes in that area may make a joint scheme to provide –

(a) for establishing a team council comprising –

(i) the team rector;

(ii) all the members of the team other than the team rector;

(iii) every assistant curate, deaconess and lay worker licensed to a parish within the team who are not members of the team;

(iv) such number of lay representatives elected by and from among the lay representatives of the

---

1 The requirements of such a scheme or order are outlined in Schedule 3, paragraph 13 of the Pastoral Measure 1983, printed at p. 154. Since the arrangements made under a pastoral scheme or order have a maximum duration of five years, a scheme made under rule 19 would normally be needed to replace those arrangements when they expired.

parochial church council of each parish in the area as may be specified in the scheme.

Provided that where the total number of persons in sub-paragraphs (ii) and (iii) above would otherwise number more than one-quarter of the total membership of the team council they may, and where those persons number more than one-third they shall select among themselves which members shall be members of the team council so that the total number of those persons shall not exceed more than one-third of the council;

(b) for the chairmanship, meetings and procedure of the team council; and

(c) subject to paragraph 19 of Schedule 2 to the Patronage (Benefices) Measure 1986 for the delegation by the parochial church council of each such parish to the team council of such functions, other than its functions as an interested party under Part I of the Pastoral Measure 1983,[1] as may be so specified and its functions under section 3 of the Priests (Ordination of Women) Measure 1993,[2] as may be so specified.

(2) Subject to the scheme and to any pastoral scheme relating to the team council made under paragraph 4(3) of Schedule 3 to the said Measure and to paragraph 19 of Schedule 2 to the Patronage (Benefices) Measure 1986, the parochial church council of any such parish may delegate to the team council such of its functions, other than its functions as an interested party under the said Part I and its functions under section 3 of the Priests (Ordination of Women) Measure 1993, as it thinks fit.

(3) The team council shall meet from time to time for the purpose of consulting together on matters of common concern.

(4) No scheme under this rule shall be valid unless approved by at least two-thirds of the persons present and voting at the annual meeting nor shall the scheme provide for it to come into operation until such date as the bishop's council and standing committee may determine being a

---

1 See p. 21 for the position of interested parties.
2 See p. 47.

date not later than the next ensuing annual meeting. Every such scheme shall on its approval be communicated to the bishop's council and standing committee of the diocesan synod which may determine –

(a)   that the scheme shall come into operation; or

(b)   that the scheme shall not come into operation; or

(c)   that the scheme shall come into operation with specified amendments, if such amendments are approved by an annual or special parochial church meeting and the scheme as amended is approved by at least two-thirds of the persons present and voting at that meeting.

(5)   A special parochial church meeting of a parish to which this rule applies may be convened for the purpose of deciding whether to join in making such a scheme, and where such a meeting is convened the foregoing provisions shall have effect with the substitution for references to the annual meeting of references to the special meeting.

(6)   Where a pastoral scheme establishing a team ministry, or an instrument of the bishop made by virtue of that scheme,[1] establishes a team council for that ministry, no scheme under this rule relating to that ministry shall provide for the scheme to come into operation until on or after the date on which the provisions of the pastoral scheme or of the instrument, as the case may be, establishing the team council cease to have effect.

(7)   A scheme under this rule may be amended or revoked by a subsequent scheme passed in accordance with the provisions of paragraph (4) of this rule.

Group councils

21. (1)   Where a pastoral scheme establishes a group ministry, the annual meetings of the parishes in the area for which the group ministry is established may make a joint scheme to provide –

---

1   The requirements of such a scheme or order are outlined in Schedule 3 paragraph 4 of the Pastoral Measure 1983, printed at p. 151. Since the arrangements made under a pastoral scheme or order have a maximum duration of five years, a scheme made under rule 20 would normally be needed to replace those arrangements when they expired.

(a) for establishing a group council comprising –

(i) all the members of the group ministry,

(ii) every assistant curate, deaconess, and lay worker licensed to any such parish, and

(iii) such number of lay representatives elected by and from among the lay members of the parochial church council of each such parish, as may be specified in the scheme;

(b) for the chairmanship, meetings and procedure of the group council; and

(c) for the delegation by the parochial church council of each such parish to the group council of such functions, other than its functions as an interested party[1] under Part I of the Pastoral Measure 1983, as may be so specified and its functions under Part II of the Patronage (Benefices) Measure 1986[2] and section 3 of the Priests (Ordination of Women) Measure 1993.[3]

(2) If the area of a group ministry includes the area of a benefice for which a team ministry is established, a scheme under this rule shall provide for the vicars in that ministry, as well as the rector, and all the other members of the team to be members of the group council.

(3) Paragraphs (2) to (7) of rule 20 shall apply in relation to a scheme under this rule as they apply in relation to a scheme under that rule with the modification that for the references to a team ministry and a team council there shall be substituted references to a group ministry and a group council respectively, except that the functions of a parochial church council under Part II of the Patronage (Benefices) Measure 1986 and section 3 of the Priests (Ordination of Women) Measure 1993 may not be delegated to a group council.

Special meetings

22. (1) In addition to the annual meeting, the minister of a parish may convene a special parochial church meeting, and he shall do so on a written representation by not less than one-third of the lay members of the parochial church

---

1 See p. 21 for the position of interested parties.
2 See p. 55.
3 See p. 47.

council; and the provisions of these rules relating to the convening and conduct of the annual meeting shall, with the necessary modifications, apply to a special parochial church meeting.

(2) All lay persons whose names are entered on the roll of the parish on the day which is twenty-one clear days before the date on which any special parochial church meeting is to be held shall be entitled to attend the meeting and to take part in its proceedings, and no other lay person shall be so entitled.

(3) A clerk in Holy Orders shall be entitled to attend any such meeting and to take part in its proceedings if by virtue of rule 6(3), (4) or (5) he would have been entitled to attend the annual meeting of the parish had it been held on the same date, and no other such clerk shall be so entitled.

Extraordinary meetings

23. (1) On a written representation made to the archdeacon by not less than one-third of the lay members of the parochial church council, or by one-tenth of the persons whose names are on the roll of the parish, and deemed by the archdeacon to have been made with sufficient cause, the archdeacon shall convene an extraordinary meeting of the parochial church council or an extraordinary parochial church meeting, and shall either take the chair himself or shall appoint a chairman to preside. The chairman, not being otherwise entitled to attend such meeting, shall not be entitled to vote upon any resolution before the meeting.

(2) In any case where the archdeacon is himself the minister, any representation under paragraph (1) of this rule shall be made to the bishop, and in any such case the references to the archdeacon in paragraph (1) of this rule shall be construed as references to the bishop, or to a person appointed by him to act on his behalf.

(3) Paragraphs (2) and (3) of rule 22 shall apply in relation to an extraordinary parochial church meeting under this rule as they apply in relation to a special parochial church meeting under that rule with the modification that for the word 'special' in paragraph (2) of that rule there shall be substituted the word 'extraordinary'.

Parts III, IV and V[1]

Part VI
APPEALS AND DISQUALIFICATIONS
Enrolments appeals

43. (1)   There shall be a right of appeal with regard to –

(a)   any enrolment, or refusal of enrolment, on the roll of a parish or the register of lay or clerical electors.

(b)   the removal of any name, or the refusal to remove any name, from the roll of a parish or the register of lay or clerical electors.

(2)   The following persons shall have a right of appeal under this rule[2] –

(a)   a person who is refused enrolment on the roll or register;

(b)   a person whose name is removed from the roll or register; or

(c)   any person whose name is entered on the roll or register who wishes to object to the enrolment or removal of the name of any other person on that roll or register.

(3)   In an appeal concerning the roll of a parish, notice of the appeal shall be given in writing to the lay chairman of the deanery synod and in an appeal concerning the register of lay or clerical electors notice of the appeal shall be given in writing to the Chairman of the House of Laity or the Chairman of the House of Clergy of the diocesan synod as the case may be.

(4)   Notice of appeal shall be given not later than fourteen days after the date of notification of the enrolment, removal or refusal or not later than 14 days after the last day of the publication (as provided by rule 2(3))[3] of a new roll or register or of a list of additions or removals from such roll or register.

(5)   In any appeal arising under this rule the chairman of the house concerned of the diocesan synod or the lay

---

1   Parts III, IV, and V of the rules (comprising rules 24 to 42) relate exclusively to deanery synods, diocesan synods and the General Synod and are here omitted.

2   Formerly the right of appeal was given to 'any person aggrieved'.

3   See p. 99.

chairman of the deanery synod, as the case may be, shall within fourteen days refer any appeal to the bishop's council and standing committee of the diocese unless within that period the appellant withdraws the appeal in writing. The said bishop's council shall appoint three or a greater number being an odd number of their lay members or clerical members as the case may be to consider and decide the appeal.

Election appeals[1]

44. (1)　There shall be a right of appeal with regard to –

    (a)　the allowance or disallowance of any vote given or tendered in an election of a churchwarden or in an election under these rules or to a body constituted under or in accordance with these rules;

    (b)　the result of any election of a churchwarden or of any election or choice held or made or purporting to be held or made under these rules, or any election or choice of members of a body constituted under or in accordance with these rules.

  (2)　The following persons shall have a right of appeal under this rule –

    (a)　an elector in the said election;

    (b)　a candidate in the said election; or

    (c)　the chairman of the house of laity or of the house of clergy of the diocesan synod . . .

  (3)　. . .

  (4)　Subject to paragraph (6) of this rule in the case of an appeal arising out of an election to the House of Laity of the General Synod or the diocesan synod notice of the appeal shall be given in writing to the chairman of the house of laity of the diocesan synod. In any other case concerning the laity, notice of the appeal shall be given in writing to the lay chairman of the deanery synod. Notices under this paragraph shall be given:

    (a)　in the case of an appeal against the allowance or disallowance of a vote, not later than fourteen days after such an allowance or disallowance;

1　Only those parts of rule 44 relating to elections at parochial level have been printed here.

(b) in the case of an appeal against the result of an election or choice, not later than fourteen days after the day on which the result is declared by the presiding officer.

(5) ...

(6) An error in the electoral roll or the registers of clerical or lay electors shall not be a ground of appeal against the result of any election unless –

(a) either it has been determined under this rule that there has been such an error or the question is awaiting determination under rule 43; and

(b) the error would or might be material to the result of the election;

(7), (8) and (9) ...

(10) In any appeal arising under this rule except an appeal arising out of an election to the House of Laity of the General Synod, the chairman of the house of laity of the diocesan synod or the lay chairman of the deanery synod, as the case may be, shall refer any appeal to the bishop's council and standing committee of the diocese who shall appoint three or a greater number, being an odd number, of their lay members to consider and decide the appeal.

(11) and (12) ...

45. For the purpose of the consideration and decision of any appeal under rules 43 and 44, the persons appointed to consider and decide the appeal –

(a) shall consider all the relevant circumstances and shall be entitled to inspect all documents and papers relating to the subject matter of the appeal and be furnished with all information respecting the same which they may require;

(b) shall give to the parties to the appeal an opportunity of appearing before them in person or through a legal or other representative;

(c) shall have power at any time to extend the time within which a notice of appeal is given;

(d) shall, unless by consent of the persons appointed the appeal is withdrawn, determine the matter at issue and, in an election appeal, shall determine whether –

(i) the person or persons whose election is complained of was or were duly elected;

    (ii) the facts complained of amount to a minor infringement of the rules which did not affect the outcome of the election in which event the appeal shall be dismissed; or

    (iii) the facts complained of amount to a procedural irregularity in the conduct of the election, but that in all the relevant circumstances the appeal shall be dismissed; or

    (iv) the election is void. The determination so certified shall be final as to the matters at issue and, in any case in which there has been no valid election, the members shall direct a fresh election to be held and shall give such directions in connection therewith as they may think necessary;

(e) shall have power at any time to consent to the withdrawal of the appeal by an appellant subject to a determination in respect of costs in accordance with paragraph (f) of this rule;

(f) shall have power to direct that any party to an appeal shall be entitled to payment of costs by any other party or by the diocesan board of finance and to direct that a party shall be responsible for the reasonable expenses of the persons appointed to hear the appeal; save that in so far as the same have not been paid by any other person, the diocesan board of finance shall pay all expenses of the persons appointed to hear the appeal provided that the said board shall first be satisfied that they are reasonable in amount.

46. . . .[1]

46A(a) A person shall be disqualified from being nominated, chosen or elected or from serving as a churchwarden, a member of a parochial church council, a district church council or any synod under these rules if he is disqualified from being a charity trustee under section 72(1) of the Charities Act 1993 and the disqualification is not for the time being subject to a general waiver by the Charity Commissioners under subsection (4) of that section or to

---

1 Rule 46 relates exclusively to vacation of membership of a deanery or diocesan synod or of the General Synod, and is here omitted.

a waiver by them under that subsection in respect of all ecclesiastical charities established for purposes relating to the parish concerned.[1]

In this paragraph 'ecclesiastical charity' has the same meaning as that assigned to that expression in the Local Government Act 1894;

(b) A person shall also be disqualified from being nominated, chosen or elected or from serving as a churchwarden or member of a parochial church council if he has been so disqualified from holding office under section 10(6) of the Incumbents (Vacation of Benefices) Measure 1977.[2]

(c) . . .

Ex-officio *membership not to disqualify for election*

47. No person shall be disqualified from being elected or chosen a member of any body under these rules by the fact that he is also a member *ex-officio* of that body; and no person shall be deemed to vacate his seat as such an elected or chosen member of any body by reason only of the fact that subsequently to his election or choice he has become a member of that body *ex-officio.*

Part VII
SUPPLEMENTARY AND INTERPRETATION
Casual vacancies

48.[3](1) Casual vacancies among the parochial representatives elected to the parochial church council or deanery synod

---

1 The Charities Act 1993, which is outside the scope of this book, provides by section 72 for the disqualification of persons who have been convicted of certain offences involving dishonesty, or who have become bankrupt, or who on other specified grounds are unfit to serve as trustees.

2 Section 10(6) of the Incumbents (Vacation of Benefices) Measure 1977, as amended by section 7 of the Incumbents (Vacation of Benefices) (Amendment) Measure 1993, enables a bishop to disqualify a parishioner who has contributed to a breakdown of the pastoral relationship within the parish from being a churchwarden of 'the parish in question'. It is not clear whether the disqualification in rule 46A (or section 2(3) of the Churchwardens Measure 2001 in similar terms) applies generally, or only to the parish where the pastoral breakdown has occurred.

3 So much of this rule as is not relevant to elections at the parochial level has been omitted.

shall be filled as soon as practicable after the vacancy has occurred. Where the annual parochial church meeting is not due to be held within the next two months following the occurrence of the vacancy, a vacancy among the parochial representatives elected to the parochial church council may be filled, and a vacancy among the parochial representatives elected to the deanery synod shall be filled, by the election by the parochial church council of a person qualified to be so elected. Returns of parochial representatives of the laity elected to fill one or more casual vacancies on the deanery synod shall be sent by the secretary of the parochial church council to the diocesan electoral registration officer and to the secretary of the deanery synod.

(2)   . . .

(3)   Subject to paragraphs (1), (2) and (6) of this rule, casual vacancies among persons elected under these rules shall be filled by elections conducted in the same manner as ordinary elections . . .

(4)   Elections to fill casual vacancies shall, where possible, be held at such times as will enable all casual vacancies among representatives of the laity who are electors to be filled at the time of every election to the House of Laity of the General Synod, but no such election shall be invalid by reason of any casual vacancies not having been so filled.

(5), (6) and (7) . . .

(8)   The preceding provisions of this rule shall apply, so far as applicable and with the necessary modifications, to the choosing of persons under these rules as it applies to the election of persons thereunder, and shall also apply to the election or choosing of members of any body constituted under or in accordance with these rules.

(9)   Any person elected or chosen to fill a casual vacancy shall hold office only for the unexpired portion of the term of office of the person in whose place he is elected or chosen.

(10) and (11) . . .

Resignations

49. Any person holding any office under these rules or being a member of any body constituted by or under these rules may resign his office or membership by notice in writing signed by him and sent or given to the secretary of the body of which he is an officer or member, as the case may be; and his resignation shall take effect on the date specified in the notice or, if no date is so specified, on the receipt of the notice by the secretary of that body.

Notices

50. Any notice or other document required or authorized to be sent or given under these rules shall be deemed to have been duly sent or given if sent through the post addressed to the person to whom it is required or authorized to be sent or given at that person's last known address.

51. . . .[1]

Revocation and variation of rules, etc.

52. Subject to the provisions of these rules any power conferred by these rules to make, approve, frame, pass or adopt any rule, order, resolution, determination, decision, appointment or scheme, or to give any consent or settle any constitution, or to prescribe the manner of doing anything, shall be construed as including a power, exercisable in a like manner and subject to the like conditions, to revoke or vary any such rule, order, resolution, determination, decision, appointment, scheme, consent or constitution, or anything so prescribed.

Special provisions

53. (1) In the carrying out of these rules in any diocese the bishop of such diocese shall have power –

(a) to make provisions for any matter not herein provided for;

(b) to appoint a person to do any act in respect of which there has been any neglect or default on the part of any person or body charged with any duty under these rules;

---

1 Rule 51, concerning constraints in elections, does not in practice apply to parochial elections. It is therefore omitted.

(c)   so far as may be necessary for the purpose of giving effect to the intention of these rules, to extend or alter the time for holding any meeting or election or to modify the procedure laid down by these rules in connection therewith provided that such power shall not be exercised in relation to the conduct of the elections referred to in rules 39 and 48 of these rules;[1]

(d)   subject to paragraph 1(c) of this rule, in any case in which any difficulties arise, to give any directions which he may consider expedient for the purpose of removing the difficulties.

(2)   The powers of the bishop under this rule shall not enable him –

(a)   to validate anything that was invalid at the time when it was done;

(b)   to give any direction that is contrary to any resolution of the General Synod.

(3)   No proceedings of any body constituted under these rules shall be invalidated by any vacancy in the membership of that body or by any defect in the qualification, election or appointment of any members thereof.

(4)   No proceedings shall be invalidated by the use of a form which differs from that prescribed by these rules if the form which has in fact been used is to a substantially similar effect. Any question as to whether the form which has been used is to a substantially similar effect shall be determined by the bishop.

(5)   In the case of an omission in any parish to prepare or maintain a roll or form or maintain a council or to hold the annual meeting, the rural dean, upon such omission being brought to his notice, shall ascertain and report to the bishop the cause thereof.

(6)   During a vacancy in an archbishopric or where by reason of illness an archbishop is unable to exercise his functions under these rules or to appoint a commissary under paragraph (10) of this rule the functions of an archbishop

---

1   Thus where there is a casual vacancy the procedure laid down in rule 48 must be followed. Rule 39, not printed here, concerns elections to the General Synod.

under these rules shall be exercisable by the other archbishop.

(7)   During a vacancy in a diocesan bishopric the functions of a diocesan bishop under these rules, including his functions as president of the diocesan synod, shall be exercisable by such person, being a person in episcopal orders, as the archbishop of the province may appoint.

(8)   Where by reason of illness a diocesan bishop is unable to exercise his functions under these rules or to appoint a commissary under paragraph (10) of this rule, the archbishop of the province may, if he thinks it necessary or expedient to do so, appoint a person in episcopal orders to exercise the functions mentioned in paragraph (7) of this rule during the period of the bishop's illness.

(9)   If a person appointed in pursuance of paragraph (7) or (8) of this rule becomes unable by reason of illness to act under the appointment, the archbishop may revoke the appointment and make a fresh one.

(10)   An archbishop or diocesan bishop may appoint a commissary and delegate to him all or any of the functions of the archbishop or bishop under these rules, but if a bishop proposes to delegate to a commissary his functions as one of the authorities which together constitute the diocesan synod he shall appoint a person in episcopal orders as commissary.

(11)   If a person appointed in pursuance of paragraph (7) or (8) of this rule, or a person to whom the functions of a bishop as president of the diocesan synod are delegated under paragraph (10) of this rule, is a member of the house of clergy of the diocesan synod, his membership of that house shall be suspended during the period for which the appointment or delegation has effect.

(12)   ... [1]

Meaning of minister, parish and other words and phrases

54. (1)   In these rules –

'actual communicant' means a person who has received Communion according to the use of the Church of England or of a Church in communion with the Church of

---

1   Rule 53(12) relates only to the diocese in Europe.

England at least three times during the twelve months preceding the date of his election or appointment being a person whose name is on the roll of a parish and is either –

(a) confirmed or ready and desirous of being confirmed; or

(b) receiving the Holy Communion in accordance with the provisions of Canon B15A paragraph 1 (b);[1]

'auditor' shall mean a person eligible as the auditor of a charity under section 43(2) of the Charities Act 1993;

'independent examiner' shall mean a person as defined in Section 43(3)(a) of the Charities Act 1993;[2]

'the Measure' means the Synodical Government Measure 1969;

'minister' means –

(a) the incumbent of a parish;

(b) a curate licensed to the charge of a parish or a minister acting as priest-in-charge of a parish in respect of which rights of presentation are suspended; and

(c) a vicar in a team ministry to the extent that the duties of a minister are assigned to him by a pastoral scheme or order or his licence from the bishop;

'parish' means –

(a) an ecclesiastical parish; and

(b) a district which is constituted a 'conventional district' for the cure of souls; and

(c) in relation to the diocese in Europe, a chaplaincy which is constituted as part of the diocese;

'public worship' means public worship according to the rites and ceremonies of the Church of England.

(2) Any reference in these rules to the laity shall be construed as a reference to persons other than clerks in Holy Orders, and the expression 'lay' in these rules shall be construed accordingly.

(3) Where a person has executed a deed of relinquishment under the Clerical Disabilities Act 1870 and the deed has been enrolled in the High Court and recorded in the

---

1   This provides that 'baptized persons who are communicant members of other Churches which subscribe to the doctrine of the Holy Trinity, and who are in good standing with their own Church' shall be admitted to the Holy Communion.

2   For 'auditors' and 'independent examiners' see p. 145 footnote 1.

registry of a diocese under that Act then, unless and until the vacation of the enrolment of the deed is recorded in such a registry under the Clerical Disabilities Act 1870 (Amendment) Measure 1934, that person shall be deemed not to be a clerk in Holy Orders for the purpose of paragraph (2) of this rule or of any other provision of these rules which refers to such a clerk.[1]

(4)   References in these rules to the cathedral church of the diocese shall include, in the case of the dioceses of London and Oxford, references to Westminster Abbey and St George's Chapel, Windsor, respectively.

(5)   If any question arises whether a Church is a Church in communion with the Church of England, it shall be conclusively determined for the purposes of these rules by the Archbishops of Canterbury and York.

(6)   In these rules words importing residence include residence of a regular nature but do not include residence of a casual nature.

(7)   Any reference herein to 'these rules' shall be construed as including a reference to the Appendices hereto.

---

1   Under the Act of 1870 referred to in the text, it is possible for an ordained minister of the Church of England, subject to certain conditions, to execute a deed of relinquishment whereby, upon the enrolment of the deed in the High Court and its being recorded in the registry of the appropriate diocese, the minister in question becomes incapable of officiating as such, and is at the same time freed from all disabilities and disqualifications to which an ordained minister is normally subject by law. The Measure of 1934, also referred to in the text, provides a procedure whereby, on the petition of the minister concerned, the enrolment of the deed of relinquishment can be vacated, and upon its vacation being recorded in the diocesan registry, the minister will revert to the same status as he had before the execution, enrolment and recording of the deed. The object of this present sub-rule (3) (introduced in 1980) is to make it clear beyond doubt that an ordained minister who has availed himself to the Act of 1870 is to be regarded as a member of the laity for all the purposes of the Rules (e.g. entry on an electoral roll, voting rights, and election as a layman to a synod or parochial church council) unless and until he reverts to his former status under the procedure provided by the Measure of 1934.

Appendix 1

Section 1

Rule 1 (2)

APPLICATION FOR ENROLMENT ON THE CHURCH ELECTORAL ROLL OF THE PARISH OF

Full name...

Preferred title (if any)...

Full address ....

....Post Code ....

I declare that

1   I am baptized and am aged 16 or over (or, become 16* on

....

2†

A   I am a member of the Church of England (or of a Church in communion with the Church of England) and am resident in the parish. □

OR

B   I am a member of the Church of England (or of a Church in communion with the Church of England) and, not being resident in the parish, I have habitually attended public worship in the parish during the period of six months prior to enrolment. □

OR

C   I am a member in good standing of a Church (not in communion with the Church of England) which subscribes to the doctrine of the Holy Trinity and also declare myself to be a member of the Church of England and I have habitually attended public worship in the parish during the period of six months prior to enrolment. □

I declare that the above answers are true and I apply for inclusion on the Church Electoral Roll of the parish.

Signed... Date............................

*Those who become 16 during the next 12 months may complete the form, and become eligible to be entered on the roll on their sixteenth birthday.

†Tick **one only** of boxes 2A, B or C.

NOTES

1. The only Churches at present in communion with the Church of England are other Anglican Churches and certain foreign Churches.

2. Membership of the electoral roll is also open to members in good standing of a Church not in communion with the Church of England which subscribes to the doctrine of the Holy Trinity where those members are also prepared to declare themselves to be members of the Church of England.

3. Every six years a new roll is prepared and those on the previous roll are informed so that they can re-apply. If you are not resident in the parish but were on the roll as an habitual worshipper and have been prevented by sickness or absence or other essential reason from worshipping for the past six months, you may write 'would' before 'have habitually attended' on the form and add 'but was prevented from doing so because . . .' and then state the reason.

4. If you have any problems over this form, please approach the clergy or lay people responsible for the parish, who will be pleased to help you.

5. In this form 'parish' means ecclesiastical parish.

Section 2

Rule 2 (1)

FORM OF NOTICE OF REVISION OF CHURCH ELECTORAL ROLL

Diocese of ....

Parish of ....

Notice is hereby given that the Church Electoral Roll of the above parish will be revised by the Parochial Church Council*, beginning

on................

*NOTE – The Revision must be completed not less than 15 days or more than 28 days before the Annual Parochial Church Meeting.

the...................day of...................200.... and ending on the...................day of...................200....

After such Revision, a copy of the roll will forthwith be exhibited for not less than 14 days on, or near to, the principal door of the Parish Church for inspection.

Under the Church Representation Rules any persons are entitled to have their names entered on the roll if they –

(i) are baptized and aged 16 or over;

(ii) have signed a form of application for enrolment;
and either

(iii) are members of the Church of England or of any Church in communion with the Church of England being resident in the parish or (not being resident in the parish) having habitually attended public worship in the parish during the six months prior to the application for enrolment;
or:

(iv) are members in good standing of a Church (not in communion with the Church of England) which subscribes to the doctrine of the Holy Trinity declaring themselves to be also members of the Church of England and having habitually attended public worship in the parish during the period of six months prior to enrolment.

Forms of application for enrolment can be obtained from the undersigned. In order to be entitled to attend the annual parochial church meeting and to take part in its proceedings forms of application for enrolment must be returned by the date shown above for the ending of the revision of the Church Electoral Roll by the Parochial Church Council. Any error discovered in the roll should at once be reported to the undersigned.

†Not less than 14 days notice should be given.

Dated this† ....day of .... 200......

....

Church Electoral Roll Officer

Address ....

NOTE: In this notice 'parish' means ecclesiastical parish.

Section 3

Rule 2 (4)

FORM OF NOTICE OF PREPARATION OF NEW ROLL

Diocese of ....

Parish of ....

NOTE – The new roll must be completed not less than 15 days or more than 28 days before the Annual Parochial Church Meeting.	Notice is hereby given that under the Church Representation Rules a new Church Electoral Roll is being prepared.* All persons who wish to have their names entered on the new roll, whether their names are entered on the present roll or not, are requested to apply for enrolment not later than.. The new roll will come into operation on...

The new roll shall be published for not less than 14 days. Forms of application for enrolment can be obtained from the undersigned. In order to be entitled to attend the annual parochial church meeting and to take part in its proceedings, forms of application for enrolment must be returned by the earlier of the dates given above.

Under the Church Representation Rules any persons are entitled to have their names entered on the roll, if they –

   (i)   are baptized and aged 16 or over;

  (ii) have signed a form of application for enrolment;
       and either

 (iii) are members of the Church of England or of any Church in communion with the Church of England being resident in the parish or (not being resident in the parish) having habitually attended public worship in the parish during the six months prior to the application for enrolment;
       or

 (iv) are members in good standing of a Church (not in communion with the Church of England) which subscribes to the doctrine of the Holy Trinity declaring themselves to be also members of the Church of England and having habitually attended public worship in the parish during the period of six months prior to enrolment.

Any error discovered in the roll should at once be reported to the undersigned.

Dated this....................................day of ....200.....

          ....

          Church Electoral Roll Officer

          Address ....

NOTE: In this notice 'parish' means ecclesiastical parish.

Section 4

Rule 7(1)

NOTICE OF ANNUAL PAROCHIAL CHURCH MEETING

Parish of...
The Annual Parochial Church Meeting will be held in.............................
on....................................day of...........................at..............................
For the election of Parochial representatives of the laity as follows –

        *To the Deanery Synod......................representatives.
        To the Parochial Church Council...................representatives.

For the appointment of Sidesmen and the Independent Examiner or
Auditor.
For the consideration of:

    (a)   A Report of changes in the roll since the last annual parochial
           church meeting.
    (b)   An Annual Report on the proceedings of the parochial church
           council and the activities of the parish generally.
    (c)   The Financial Statements of the Council for the year ending on
           31st December immediately preceding the meeting audited or
           independently examined;
    (d)   A Report upon the fabric, goods and ornaments of the church or
           churches of the parish;
    (e)   A Report on the proceedings of the Deanery Synod;
and other matters of parochial or general Church interest.

NOTES

1. All persons whose names are entered upon the Church Electoral Roll
   of the parish (and such persons only) are entitled to vote at the
   election of parochial representatives of the laity.
2. Subject to the provisions of rule 14(3)(c), a person is qualified to be
   elected a parochial representative of the laity if –
       (a)   his name is entered on the Church Electoral Roll of the parish;
       (b)   he is an actual communicant which means that he has received
              Communion according to the use of the Church of England or
              of a Church in communion with the Church of England at least
              three times during the twelve months preceding the date of the
              election; and
       (c)   he is of eighteen years or upwards (for election to the deanery
              synod) or of sixteen years or upwards (for election to the
              parochial church council); and
       (d)   he is not disqualified as referred to in paragraph 3 of these Notes.
3. (a)   A person shall be disqualified from being nominated, chosen or
              elected or from serving as a churchwarden, a member of a
              parochial church council, a district church council or any synod

under these rules if he is disqualified from being a charity trustee under section 72(1) of the Charities Act 1993 and the disqualification is not for the time being subject to a general waiver by the Charity Commissioners under subsection (4) of that section or to a waiver by them under that subsection in respect of all ecclesiastical charities established for purposes relating to the parish concerned.

In this paragraph 'ecclesiastical charity' has the same meaning as that assigned to that expression in the Local Government Act 1894;

(b) A person shall also be disqualified from being nominated, chosen or elected or from serving as a churchwarden or member of a parochial church council if he has been so disqualified from holding office under section 10(6) of the Incumbents (Vacation of Benefices) Measure 1977.

4. Any person whose name is on the electoral roll may be appointed as a sidesman.

5. **A scheme is in operation in this parish which provides that any person entitled to vote in the elections of parochial representatives of the laity to the parochial church council or to the deanery synod or to both that council and that synod may make application on the appropriate form to the undersigned for a postal vote. The completed form must be received before the commencement of the Annual Parochial Church Meeting.

Signed .... †Minister of the parish.

---

*Include where applicable.

**This paragraph should be deleted if no scheme for postal voting is in operation in the parish.

†Or 'Vice-Chairman of the Parochial Church Council' as the case may be (see rule 7(3) of the Church Representation Rules).

NOTE: In this notice 'parish' means an ecclesiastical parish.

Section 4A

Rule 11(2)

APPLICATION FOR POSTAL VOTE

Parish of ....

I (full Christian name and surname) ....

of (full postal address) ....

declare that my name is entered on the church electoral roll of the above parish and I hereby make application for a postal vote in any elections to which postal voting applies to be held at the forthcoming annual parochial church meeting for the parish. The voting paper should be sent or delivered to me at the above address OR★ at the following address

....

Dated .... 200...........

Signed ....

★Delete as appropriate.

The remaining sections of this Appendix relate only to diocesan synods and are here omitted.

Appendix 2

Rule 15

GENERAL PROVISIONS RELATING TO
PAROCHIAL CHURCH COUNCILS

Officers of the council

1.　(a)　The minister of the parish shall be chairman of the parochial church council (hereinafter referred to as 'the council').

　　(b)　A lay member of the council shall be elected as vice-chairman of the council.

　　(c)　During the vacancy of the benefice or when the chairman is incapacitated by absence or illness or any other cause or when the minister invites him to do so the vice-chairman of the council shall act as chairman and have all the powers vested in the chairman.

　　(d)　(i)　The council may appoint one of their number to act as secretary of the council. Failing such appointment the office of secretary shall be discharged by some other fit person who shall not thereby become a member of the council, provided that such person may be co-opted to the council in accordance with the provisions of rule 14(1)(h);[1]

　　　　(ii)　where a person other than a member of the council is appointed to act as secretary, that person may be paid such remuneration (if any) as the council deems appropriate provided that such person shall not be eligible to be a member of the council.

　　　　(iii)　The secretary shall have charge of all documents relating to the current business of the council except that, unless he is the electoral roll officer, he shall not have charge of the roll. He shall be responsible for keeping the minutes, shall record all resolutions passed by the council and shall keep the secretary of the diocesan synod and deanery synod informed as to his name and address.

　　(e)　(i)　The council may appoint one or more of their number to act as treasurer solely or jointly. Failing such appointment, the office of treasurer shall be discharged by some other fit person or either –

　　　　　　by such of the churchwardens as are members of the council or, if there is only one such churchwarden, by that churchwarden solely; or
　　　　　　by some other fit person who shall not thereby

1　See p. 113.

become a member of the council, provided that such person may be co-opted to the council in accordance with the provisions of rule 14(1)(h).

(ii) where a person other than a member of the council is appointed to act as treasurer that person may be paid such remuneration (if any) as the council deems appropriate provided that such person shall not be eligible to be a member of that council.

(f) The council shall appoint an electoral roll officer, who may but need not be a member of the council and may be the secretary and if he is not a member may pay to him such remuneration as it shall think fit. He shall have charge of the roll.

(g) If an independent examiner or auditor to the council is not appointed by the annual meeting or if an independent examiner or auditor[1] appointed by the annual meeting is unable or unwilling to act, an independent examiner or auditor (who shall not be a member of the council) shall be appointed by the council for a term of office ending at the close of the next annual meeting. The remuneration (if any) of the independent examiner or auditor shall be paid by the council.

(h) For the purposes of this paragraph, where a special cure of souls in respect of a parish has been assigned to a vicar in a team ministry, or where there has been no such assignment

---

1 An auditor is defined in rule 54 as 'a person eligible as the auditor of a charity under section 43(2) of the Charities Act 1993'. An auditor is required where the annual gross income or expenditure exceeds £250,000. Where it is intended to appoint an auditor of the accounts of a parish, he should be asked to confirm that his professional qualifications allow him to act as the auditor of a charity for the purposes of the Charities Act 1993. If the annual gross income or expenditure falls between £10,000 and £250,000, it is sufficient for an independent examiner to be appointed. Such a person is defined in rule 54 by reference to section 43(3) of the Charities Act 1993 as an 'independent person who is reasonably believed . . . to have the requisite ability and practical experience to carry out a competent examination of the accounts'. There is no duty under the Charities Act 1993 to appoint an independent examiner where the annual income or expenditure is less than £10,000. Paragraph 4(g) above appears, nonetheless, to make the appointment of an auditor or independent examiner mandatory in all cases. Further guidance concerning the requirements of the Charities Act 1993 in relation to parish accounts is to be found in the booklet *The Charities Act '93 and the PCC* published by the Central Board of Finance of the Church of England. Reference should also be made to the Church Accounting Regulations 1997, which set out in detail the requirements for the preparation and audit of accounts. Both publications are available from the Church House Bookshop, 31 Great Smith Street, London SW1P 3BN.

but a special responsibility for pastoral care in respect of the parish has been assigned to a member of the team under section 20(8A) of the Pastoral Measure 1983, that vicar or that member, as the case may be, shall be deemed to be the minister unless incapacitated by absence or illness or any other cause, in which case the rector in the team ministry shall be deemed to be the minister.

Meetings of the council

2. The council shall hold not less than four meetings in each year. Meetings shall be convened by the chairman and if not more than four meetings are held they shall be at quarterly intervals so far as possible.

Power to call meetings

3. The chairman may at any time convene a meeting of the council. If he refuses or neglects to do so within seven days after a requisition for that purpose signed by not less than one-third of the members of the council has been presented to him those members may forthwith convene a meeting.

Notices relating to meetings[1]

4. (a) Except as provided in paragraph 8 of this Appendix, at least ten clear days before any meeting of the council notice thereof specifying the time and place of the intended meeting and signed by or on behalf of the chairman of the council or the persons convening the meeting shall be posted at or near the principal door of every church, or building licensed for public worship in the parish.

   (b) Not less than seven days before the meeting a notice thereof specifying the time and place of the meeting signed by or on behalf of the secretary shall be posted or delivered to every member of the council or, if the member has authorized the use of an electronic mail address, to that address. Such notice shall contain the agenda of the meeting including any motion or other business proposed by any member of the council of which notice has been received by the secretary. The notice required by this sub-paragraph shall not be required for a council meeting immediately following the annual parochial church meeting being a council meeting which has been called solely for the purpose of appointing or

---

1   See p. 124–5 concerning special and extraordinary meetings.

electing any officers of the council or the members of the standing committee thereof provided that the notice required by sub-paragraph (a) hereof has been given.

(c)   If for some good and sufficient reason the chairman, vice-chairman and secretary, or any two of them, consider that a convened meeting should be postponed, notice shall be given to every member of the council specifying a recon-vened time and place within fourteen days of the post-poned meeting.

Chairman at meetings

5.   Subject to the provisions of rules 22 and 23 the chair at a meeting of the council shall be taken –
     (a)   by the chairman of the council, if he is present;
     (b)   if the chairman is not present, by the clerk in Holy Orders, licensed to or with permission to officiate in the parish duly authorized by the bishop with the clerk's agreement, following a joint application by the minister of the parish and the council or, if the benefice is vacant, by the council for the purposes of this sub-paragraph;
     (c)   if neither the chairman of the council nor the clerk mentioned in sub-paragraph (b) above is present, by the vice-chairman of the council;
     Provided that at any such meeting the chairman presiding shall, if he thinks it expedient to do so or the meeting so resolves, vacate the chair either generally or for the purposes of any business in which he has a personal interest or for any other particular business.

     Should none of the persons mentioned above be available to take the chair for any meeting or for any particular item on the agenda during a meeting then the vice-chairman of the council shall take the chair or, if he is not present, a chairman shall be chosen by those members present from among their number and the person so chosen shall preside for that meeting or for that particular item.

Quorum and agenda

6.   No business shall be transacted at any meeting of the council unless at least one-third of the members are present thereat and no business which is not specified in the agenda shall be trans-acted at any meeting except by the consent of three-quarters of the members present at the meeting.

Order of business

7. The business of a meeting of the council shall be transacted in the order set forth in the agenda unless the council by resolution otherwise determine.

Short notice for emergency meetings

8. In case of sudden emergency or other special circumstance requiring immediate action by the council a meeting may be convened by the chairman of the council at not less than three clear days' notice in writing to the members of the council but the quorum for the transaction of any business at such meetings shall be a majority of the then existing members of the council and no business shall be transacted at such meeting except as is specified in the notice convening the meeting.

Place of meetings

9. The meeting of the council shall be held at such place as the council may direct or in the absence of such direction as the chairman may direct.

Vote of majority to decide

10. The business of the council shall be decided by a majority of the members present and voting thereon.

Casting vote

11. In the case of an equal division of votes the chairman of the meeting shall have a second or casting vote.

Minutes

12. (a) The names of the members present at any meeting of the council shall be recorded in the minutes.

 (b) If one-fifth of the members present and voting on any resolution so require, the minutes shall record the names of the members voting for and against that resolution.

 (c) Any member of the council shall be entitled to require that the minutes shall contain a record of the manner in which his vote was cast on any resolution.

 (d) Minutes of meetings of the council shall be available to all members of the council. The members shall also have access to past minutes which the chairman and vice-chairman jointly determine to be relevant to current council business.

 (e) The independent examiner or auditor of the council's accounts, the bishop and the archdeacon and any person authorized by one of them in writing shall have access to the approved minutes of council meetings without the authority of the council.

(f) Other persons whose names are on the church electoral roll may have access to the approved minutes of council meetings held after the annual parochial church meeting in 1995 except any minutes deemed by the council to be confidential.

(g) Other persons may have access to the minutes of council meetings only in accordance with a specific authorization of the council provided that where minutes have been deposited in the diocesan record office pursuant to the Parochial Registers and Records Measure 1978, the authorization of the council may be dispensed with.

Adjournment

13. Any meeting of the council may adjourn its proceedings to such time and place as may be determined at such meeting.

Standing committee

14. (a) The council shall have a standing committee consisting of not less than five persons. The minister and such of the churchwardens as are members of the council shall be *ex-officio* members of the standing committee, and the council shall by resolution appoint at least two other members of the standing committee from among its own members and may remove any person so appointed. Unless removed from office, the appointed members shall hold office from the date of their appointment until the conclusion of the next annual meeting of the parish.

(b) The standing committee shall have power to transact the business of the council between the meetings thereof subject to any directions given by the council.

Other committees

15. The council may appoint other committees for the purpose of the various branches of church work in the parish, and may include therein persons who are not members of the council. The minister shall be a member of all committees *ex-officio.*

16. An independent examiner or auditor of the council's financial statements shall –

(a) have a right of access with respect to books, documents or other records (however kept) which relate to the said financial statements;

(b) have a right to require information and explanations from past or present treasurers or members of the council and, in case of default, the independent examiner or auditor may apply to the Charity Commissioners for an order for directions pursuant to section 44(2) of the Charities Act 1993 or any statutory modification thereof for the time being in force.

Validity of proceedings

17. No proceedings of the council shall be invalidated by any vacancy in the membership of the council or by any defect in the qualification or election of any member thereof.

Interpretation

18. Any question arising on the interpretation of this Appendix shall be referred to the bishop of the diocese and any decision given by him or by any person appointed by him on his behalf shall be final.[1]

---

1   It has been held that this provision does not oust the jurisdiction of the ordinary courts on a question of interpretation.

PROVISIONS OF PASTORAL MEASURE 1983 AS TO CHURCH MEETINGS AND COUNCILS IN CERTAIN CASES[1]

SCHEDULE 3

4. (1) Where a pastoral scheme establishes a team ministry, the scheme, or the bishop's licence of any vicar in the team ministry, may assign to any such vicar the duties or a share in the duties of the chairmanship of the annual parochial church meeting and the parochial church council of the parish or any of the parishes in the area of the benefice for which the team ministry is established, and other duties of the minister of the parish under the Church Representation Rules,[2] or a share in such other duties, and the said Rules shall have effect accordingly:

Provided that, if the said duties of chairmanship are to be shared, the arrangements shall be such that the chairman on any occasion is determined in advance so that, in his absence, the vice-chairman[3] of the parochial church council shall take the chair in accordance with the said Rules.

(2) Where a pastoral scheme establishes a team ministry for the area of a benefice which comprises a parish in which there are two or more churches or places of worship, the scheme may make provision, or authorize the bishop by instrument under his hand with the concurrence of the rector to make provision –

(a) for ensuring due representation of the congregation of each such church or place of worship on the parochial church council of the parish,

(b) for the election of a district church council for any district in the parish in which such church or place of worship is situated and for the constitution, chairmanship and procedure of that council,

(c) for the functions of the parochial church council of the parish which must or may be delegated to the district church council,

---

1 The provisions in question are those contained in Schedule 3, paragraph 4 (relating to team and group ministries), paragraph 12 (relating to new parishes), and paragraph 13 (relating to united benefices and benefices held in plurality). The text of all three paragraphs is here set out.

2 See the parts of the Church Representation Rules set out at p. 103 *et seq.*

3 The vice-chairman is always a member of the laity: Church Representation Rules, Appendix 2, paragraph 1(b) (p. 144).

(d)   for the election or choice of deputy churchwardens for such church or place of worship and for the functions of churchwardens of the parish which must or may be delegated to the deputy churchwardens,

being provisions to the same effect as those which may be made by a scheme under the Church Representation Rules in the like case.

In this sub-paragraph 'place of worship' means a building or part of a building licensed for public worship according to the rites and ceremonies of the Church of England.

(3)   Where a pastoral scheme establishes a team ministry for the area of a benefice which comprises more than one parish, the scheme may make provision, or authorize the bishop by instrument under his hand with the concurrence of the rector to make provision –

(a)   for the establishment of a team council,

(b)   for the chairmanship, meetings and procedure of the team council, and

(c)   subject to paragraph 19 of schedule 2 to the Patronage (Benefices) Measure 1986, for the functions of the parochial church council of each parish in the area which must or may be delegated to the team council,

being provisions to the same effect as those which may be made by a scheme under the Church Representation Rules in the like case.

(4)   Where a pastoral scheme establishes a group ministry, the scheme may make provision, or authorize the bishop by instrument under his hand with the concurrence of all the members of the group to make provision,

(a)   for the establishment of a group council,

(b)   for the chairmanship, meetings and procedure of the group council, and

(c)   for the functions of the parochial church council of each parish in the area for which the group ministry is established which must or may be delegated to the group council,

being provisions to the same effect as those which may be made by a scheme under the Church Representation Rules in the like case.

(5)   Any provisions which are included in a pastoral scheme or the bishop's instrument by virtue of sub-paragraph

(2), (3) or (4) shall cease to have effect[1] at the expiration of such period as may be specified in the scheme or instrument, as the case may be, being a period which does not exceed five years from the date of the establishment of the team ministry or group ministry to which the pastoral scheme or instrument relates, and that period may not be extended or renewed by a subsequent scheme or instrument of the bishop.

(6) Any provisions which were included in a pastoral scheme or bishop's instrument by virtue of sub-paragraph (2) or (4), as originally enacted,[2] shall cease to have effect at the expiration of whichever of the following periods last expires, that is to say, the period of five years beginning with the date of the establishment of the team ministry or group ministry to which the scheme or instrument relates and the period of three years beginning with the date on which this Measure comes into operation.

12. (1) A pastoral scheme which creates a new parish may make provision, or authorize the bishop by instrument under his hand to make provision, for ensuring that the congregation of every church or place of worship in the new parish will have its own elected representatives of the laity on the parochial church council of that parish.

(2) Any provision included in a pastoral scheme or the bishop's instrument by virtue of sub-paragraph (1) shall cease to have effect at the expiration of such period as may be specified in the scheme or instrument, as the case may be, being a period which does not exceed five years beginning with the date on which the new parish comes into being, and that period may not be extended or renewed by a subsequent pastoral scheme or instrument of the bishop.[3]

(3) Any such provision shall have effect notwithstanding anything in the Church Representation Rules.

(4) Without prejudice to any general rule of law relating to

---

1 When the provisions mentioned in sub-paragraph 5 cease to have effect, the normal procedure would be to replace them with a scheme made under rules 18, 20 or 21 of the Church Representation Rules; see p. 118 *et seq.*

2 i.e. as Schedule 3, paragraph 3, sub-paragraphs (2) and (4) of the Pastoral Measure 1968.

3 Once the period of up to five years has expired, the position is governed by the Church Representation Rules; see p. 117 *et seq.*

parochial church councils, the powers, duties and liabilities set out in section 4(1)(ii) of the Parochial Church Councils (Powers) Measure 1956[1] shall continue to apply to any church which was formerly a parish church and becomes a chapel-of-ease as the result of a pastoral scheme or order, and to the churchyard of any such church, except so far as the scheme or order otherwise provides.

13. (1) Where a pastoral scheme provides for two or more parishes to be comprised in the area of a single benefice or a pastoral scheme or order provides for two or more benefices to be held in plurality, the scheme or order may make provision, or authorize the bishop by instrument under his hand with the concurrence of the incumbent of the benefice or benefices to make provision –

 (a) for establishing a joint parochial church council for all or some of the parishes of the benefice or benefices;

 (b) for the chairmanship, meetings and procedure of that council; and

 (c) for the functions of the parochial church council of any such parish which must or may be delegated to the joint parochial church council,

being provisions to the same effect as those which may be made by a scheme under the Church Representation Rules in the like case.

(2) Subject to sub-paragraph (4), any provisions which are included in a pastoral scheme or order or the bishop's instrument by virtue of sub-paragraph (1) shall cease to have effect[2] at the expiration of such period as may be specified in the scheme, order or instrument, being a period which does not exceed five years from the date on which the scheme or order, as the case may be, came into operation, and that period may not be extended or renewed by a subsequent pastoral scheme, pastoral order or instrument of the bishop.

---

1 See p. 164.
2 When the provisions mentioned in sub-paragraph (2) cease to have effect, the normal procedure would be to replace them with a scheme made under rule 19 of the Church Representation Rules; see p. 119.

(3) Subject to sub-paragraph (4), any provisions which were included in a pastoral scheme or order by virtue of this paragraph as originally enacted,[1] shall cease to have effect at whichever of the following periods last expires, that is to say, the period of five years beginning with the date of the establishment of the joint parochial church council to which the scheme or order relates and the period of three years beginning with the date on which this Measure comes into operation.

(4) Where the provisions of a pastoral scheme or order for the holding of benefices in plurality are terminated under section 18(2), any provision of a pastoral scheme or order or the bishop's instrument establishing a joint parochial church council for all or some of the parishes of those benefices and the other provisions thereof affecting that council shall cease to have effect on the date on which the first mentioned provisions cease to have effect.

---

1 i.e. Schedule 3, paragraph 13 of the Pastoral Measure 1968.

11 Powers and Responsibilities of Parochial Church Councils

INTRODUCTION

While Chapter 10 dealt with the membership and constitution of a parochial church council, the following paragraphs concern its functions and legal powers. Included under separate headings are various legal requirements which have in recent years assumed importance, and which in practice fall within the council's remit.

To the council have been transferred (amongst other powers) all the powers which, until the coming into force of the Parochial Church Councils (Powers) Measure 1921, were vested in the churchwardens in relation to (a) the financial affairs of the church, (b) the care, maintenance and insurance of the fabric of the church and its goods and ornaments, and (c) the care and maintenance of the churchyard.

The powers conferred on the council, as distinct from those transferred to it, include the power to acquire, manage and administer property for ecclesiastical purposes affecting the parish, power to frame an annual budget of moneys required for maintenance of church work, power to levy and collect a voluntary church rate for any church purpose, and power to make representations to the bishop with regard to any matter affecting the welfare of the church in the parish.

The council is also given power, jointly with the incumbent, to appoint and dismiss the parish clerk and sexton and to determine the salaries and conditions of service of these officers, and to determine the objects to which money collected in church are to be allocated.

All the powers so far mentioned are contained in the Parochial Church Councils (Powers) Measure 1956.[1] There follow some

---

1   This Measure is set out at p. 162 *et seq.*

examples of powers and functions conferred on parochial church councils by various other legislative provisions:

1. A council is entitled to object to a proposal under the Parsonages Measure 1938 for the sale or pulling down of a residence
   · house belonging to the benefice, or for the erection or purchase of a new residence house. Any such objection must be considered by the Church Commissioners before consenting to the proposal.
2. A parochial church council is given certain rights and duties on the occurrence of a vacancy in the benefice by the Patronage (Benefices) Measure 1986. These are considered in detail in Chapter 6.
3. The council has an important voice in any decisions (a) as to the use of forms of service authorized by the Church of England (Worship and Doctrine) Measure 1974 and the canons made thereunder; (b) as to the use in Prayer Book services of any version of Scripture authorized by or under the Prayer Book (Versions of the Bible) Measure 1965; (c) under Canons B11 and B14A as to the holding of services elsewhere than in the parish church; and (d) under Canon B8, as to any change of practice in regard to the vesture worn by a minister at divine service. These matters are dealt with on pp. 30–4.
4. Under the Pastoral Measure 1983, the parochial church council of any parish which is liable to be affected by a proposed pastoral scheme or order is an 'interested party' whose views must be ascertained, and to whom an opportunity must be given of meeting the Pastoral Committee or a subcommittee or representative thereof. On the preparation of the draft scheme or order by the Church Commissioners, a copy of the draft must be sent to the council, together with a notice stating that written representations with respect to it must be made within a specified time, not being less than 28 days.
5. Under the Sharing of Church Buildings Act 1969, when the Church of England is concerned in a 'sharing agreement' relating to any church building, the parochial church council of the parish in which the building is situated is a necessary party to the agreement.
6. Where an incumbent or a vicar in a team ministry is subject to the age-limit provisions of the Ecclesiastical Offices (Age Limit) Measure 1975, the consent of the council is necessary to any

extension of his tenure of office beyond the normal retiring age of 70.

7. Under the Incumbents (Vacation of Benefices Measure) 1977, a two-thirds majority of the lay members of a parochial church council may make a request for an inquiry under the Measure into the pastoral position in the parish (see p. 35).

8. Section 6 of the Care of Churches and Ecclesiastical Jurisdiction Measure 1991 transferred to the parochial church council the responsibility for the trees in a churchyard which it was liable to maintain.

9. Under the Clergy Discipline Measure 2003 a meeting attended by at least two-thirds of the lay members may, by a majority of not less than two-thirds of those present and voting, resolve to make a complaint through a nominated person against a priest or deacon (see p. 10).

10. Under Canons F1 to F14, the parochial church council is charged with the provision of certain requisites of divine service. The articles so prescribed include a font, a holy table, communion plate, communion linen, surplices for the minister, a reading desk and a pulpit, seats for the congregation, church bells, a large Bible and Prayer Book and a pulpit Bible, an alms box, register books, and a service book and banns book. The council is also charged by the same canons with the general duty of the care and repair of all churches, chapels and churchyards within the parish.

DATA PROTECTION

The requirements of the Data Protection Act 1998 are both complex and burdensome. The church electoral roll and the parish registers, as public documents, are exempted from the Act. Other records kept for parish use may, however, be caught by its provisions, which apply to both computerized and manual filing systems. Thus, for example, an alphabetically arranged paper file containing personal information such as names, addresses, religious beliefs and confidential details of parishioners would be subject to the Act.

It is desirable for a parish so to arrange its records as to fall outside, as far as possible, the scope of the data protection legislation. The appointment of a person to keep a check on compliance with the law may be helpful. Where the Act does apply, registration with the Office of the Information Commissioner by the data controller (usually the parochial church council) is mandatory.

Whether subject to registration or not, personal information must be kept on behalf of the parish in accordance with the data protection principles. Those principles most obviously relevant at parish level are that the data must be held fairly and lawfully; it must be accurate and kept up to date; and it must not be kept longer than is necessary. Precautions have to be taken against unauthorized use or accidental loss.

Normally any person about whom personal information is held has a legal right of access to that information

DISABILITY DISCRIMINATION

Sections 19 and 21 of the Disability Discrimination Act 1995 forbid a provider of any place to which the public has access from discriminating against a disabled person, in particular in relation to access to a building and the provision of facilities such as sound reinforcement. This duty is, however, subject to the qualification that the provider need do no more than is reasonable in the circumstances to avoid discrimination.

The practical effect of the Act is to require a parochial church council actively to make arrangements in the church, churchyard and any other premises which it controls to prevent discrimination against disabled people. Disability in this context is not limited to restricted mobility; included, among many others, are impairments of sight or hearing.

Compliance with the Act is best achieved by carrying out a periodic audit to ascertain how user-friendly are the arrangements for the disabled. Many dioceses supply prepared forms for this purpose, and there is often a specialist member of the Diocesan Advisory Committee who is able to assist parishes. Once the audit is completed, alterations such as ramps, handrails or sound amplification may be found necessary. Most alterations of this kind will require a faculty.

The issue of reasonableness has always to be borne in mind. What is reasonably required in terms of access to the nave or chancel may be inappropriate in relation to a crypt or tower. The degree of interference with historic fabric is also relevant when considering what is reasonable. Where there is a possible conflict between the requirements of the Act and the conservation of historic buildings, amenity bodies such as English Heritage and the Society for the Protection of Ancient Buildings are able to give good advice.

HEALTH AND SAFETY

The requirements of the Health and Safety at Work Act 1974 and the numerous regulations associated with it are wide-ranging. Normally they have a direct effect upon parish churches only when building works of some sort are being carried out. In such cases the church architect or surveyor, and the responsible contractor, will attend to safety matters, among them compliance with the Construction (Design and Management) Regulations 1994.

Two aspects of health and safety call for particular attention. The first is that any kind of building maintenance at potentially dangerous levels above ground, which will include gutter clearance or the replacement of light bulbs, may well fall within the Work at Height Regulations 2005. Safety inspectors have invoked these Regulations in requiring scaffolding to be used in place of traditional ladders, the safety of which has become suspect. Safe means have now to be devised for dealing with work at heights. A group of parishes may find it economical to acquire a tower scaffold and to share it between them.

The second matter concerns the presence of asbestos in buildings. During the twentieth century this material was commonly used in buildings and is to be found in roofing, insulation and the lagging of heating systems. It was also used in the blowers of pipe organs. Asbestos is highly dangerous when it becomes airborne and is inhaled as dust. When detected, asbestos disposal must be carried out by a licensed contractor.

Regulation 4 of the Control of Asbestos at Work Regulations 2002 places a duty on the controller of non-domestic premises to manage any asbestos present there. In relation to a church and any other building under its control, the duty rests with the parochial church council.

The primary requirement under Regulation 4 is to conduct an assessment to see whether any asbestos is present. If asbestos is found, its location must be recorded on a plan and the hazard which it poses must be evaluated. Expert advice, initially from the church architect or surveyor, should be sought concerning the risks arising from the asbestos and further compliance with legal requirements.

TESTING OF CHURCHYARD MONUMENTS

Anxieties about the stability of churchyard monuments has led to calls for their periodic inspection. Primary responsibility for the safety of a monument rests with its owner (in law, the person who set it up and, after that person's death, the heirs of the deceased to whom the monument relates). Those having control of the churchyard may also be liable to persons injured by a defect in it. In the case of churchyards still open for burial, the parochial church council has the necessary control and should conduct the tests. Closed churchyards[1] are usually inspected for safety by the local authority responsible for their maintenance.

Testing ought ideally to be carried out annually and a record kept of monuments found to be unstable, either on hand testing or when tested mechanically with a device such as a 'topple tester'. (Where a 'topple tester' is used, it should be calibrated to 35 kilograms or less.)

Debate as to the best way of dealing with dangerous monuments is continuing. Laying them flat may instelf create trapping hazards. Alternative strategies include propping stones up with stakes, or marking them with warning signs.

Whenever possible, the owner of the monument should be given the opportunity to rectify the fault before the monument is displaced. Displacement needs to be authorized by a faculty. Many diocesan chancellors permit comprehensive faculties to be issued covering both inspection and making safe.

---

1   See p. 165, note 2 for closed churchyards.

THE PAROCHIAL CHURCH COUNCILS (POWERS)
MEASURE 1956 (AS AMENDED) WITH NOTES

A Measure to consolidate with amendments certain enactments relating to parochial church councils and parochial charities (5th July 1956).

Definitions

1. In this Measure –

    'Council' means a parochial church council;

    'Diocesan Authority' means the Diocesan Board of Finance or any existing or future body appointed by the Diocesan Synod to act as trustees of diocesan trust property;

    'Minister' and 'Parish' have the meanings respectively assigned to them in the Rules for the Representation of the Laity;[1]

    'Relevant date' means the first day of July, 1921.[2]

General functions of council

2.[3] (1) It shall be the duty of the minister and the parochial church council to consult together on matters of general concern and importance to the parish.

   (2) The functions of parochial church councils shall include –

   (a) co-operation with the minister in promoting in the parish the whole mission of the Church, pastoral, evangelistic, social and ecumenical;[4]

---

1   These rules have been replaced by the Church Representation Rules. The relevant definitions are now contained in rule 54 of the last-mentioned rules (p. 134).

2   The date of the coming into force of the original Parochial Church Councils (Powers) Measure 1921, which this Measure has replaced.

3   This section was substituted by the Synodical Government Measure 1969 for the original section 2, which read: 'It shall be the primary duty of the council in every parish to co-operate with the minister in the initiation, conduct and development of church work both within the parish and outside.' The new section, in accordance with the general scheme of synodical government, lays greater emphasis on the part to be played by the laity.

4   It is permissible for the council to apply a reasonable part of its general funds for any purposes which will further 'the whole mission of the Church' as so described, e.g. by subscriptions to charities. Having regard in particular to the word 'social', it is considered that subscriptions may properly be made to charities for the relief of sick, poor or other necessitous persons, even though the objects of such charities are not specifically religious.

(b)   the consideration and discussion of matters concerning the Church of England or any other matters of religious or public interest, but not the declaration of the doctrine of the Church on any question;

(c)   making known and putting into effect any provision made by the diocesan synod or the deanery synod, but without prejudice to the powers of the council on any particular matter;

(d)   giving advice to the diocesan synod and the deanery synod on any matter referred to the council;

(e)   raising such matters as the council consider appropriate with the diocesan synod or deanery synod.

(3)   In the exercise of its functions the parochial church council shall take into consideration any expression of opinion by any parochial church meeting.

Council to be a body corporate

3.   Every council shall be a body corporate by the name of the parochial church council of the parish for which it is appointed and shall have perpetual succession.[1] Any act of the council may be signified by an instrument executed pursuant to a resolution of the council and under the hands or if an instrument under seal is required under the hands and seals of the chairman presiding and two other members of the council present at the meeting at which such resolution is passed.

Powers vested in council as successor to certain other bodies

4.   (1)   Subject to the provisions of any Act or Measure passed after the relevant date and to anything lawfully done under such provisions, the council of every parish shall have –

(i)   The like powers duties and liabilities as immediately before the relevant date, the vestry[2] of such parish had

---

1   These words give the council a corporate existence independent of the personnel comprised in it. It is a separate entity recognized by law, and exists as such for all time.

2   The vestry was a parochial body which included the incumbent or curate-in-charge, and the persons of both sexes who were rated for the relief of the poor in respect of the parish, whether resident therein or not, and the occupiers of hereditaments so rated. It originally had both civil and ecclesiastical functions, but it was deprived of practically all its civil functions by statute many years ago. Immediately before the coming into force of the Parochial Church Council (Powers) Measure 1921, its principal ecclesiastical functions were the election of churchwardens and other matters specified (whether as included in or as excluded from the transfer of functions to the council) in this present paragraph (i).

with respect to the affairs of the church except as regards the election of churchwardens and sidesmen[1] and as regards the administration of ecclesiastical charities[2] but including the power of presentation to the benefice of such parish if the right to present thereto was vested in or in trust for the parishioners and the power of making any voluntary church rate.[3]

(ii) The like powers duties and liabilities as, immediately before the relevant date, the churchwardens of such parish had with respect to –

(a) The financial affairs of the Church including the collection and administration of all moneys raised for church purposes and the keeping of accounts in relation to such affairs and moneys;[4]

(b) The care maintenance preservation and insur-

---

1   As to the modern law relating to the appointment of churchwardens, see Chapter 7. As to the election of sidesmen by the annual parochial church meeting, see p. 108.

2   Broadly speaking, this expression covers every charity for the religious purposes of any church or denomination. The administration of any such charity which was originally vested in the vestry will in most instances by now have been transferred to some other persons or body by a scheme made by the court or the Charity Commissioners.

3   The right to enforce or compel the payment of a church rate in any ecclesiastical or other court was taken away by the Compulsory Church Rates Abolition Act 1868; but the same Act expressly reserved the power for vestries, in both ancient and modern parishes and districts to make and assess a church rate, on the footing that payment by the person on whom it is assessed is voluntary. A 'church rate' is defined for this purpose as a rate for ecclesiastical purposes, i.e. for the 'building, rebuilding, enlargement and repair of any church or chapel, and any purpose to which by common or ecclesiastical law a church rate is applicable, or any of such purposes'.

The Act did not affect the recovery of church rates specially imposed by any private or local Act of Parliament, where the power to levy the rate was conferred for valuable consideration (such as the extinguishment of tithes or customary payments) of a nature specified in the Act. Such rates are still enforceable.

In practice, the power conferred by the Act to make a voluntary church rate was never of much value in most parishes, and its use at the present day is rare. But for what it is worth it is now vested in the parochial church council. When it is proposed to exercise it, it would appear that it is the duty of the churchwardens to prepare an estimate of the sum required and to lay it before the council, in the same way as they formerly prepared such an estimate and laid it before the vestry. After the churchwardens have done this they are relieved of responsibility.

4   As to money collected in church, see section 7(iv) and note thereto.

ance of the fabric of the church and the goods and ornaments thereof;[1]

(c) The care and maintenance of the churchyard (open or closed), and the power of giving a certificate under the provisions of section 18 of the Burial Act 1855, with the like powers as immediately before the relevant date were possessed by the churchwardens to recover the cost of maintaining a closed churchyard.[2] Provided that nothing herein contained shall affect the property[3] of the churchwardens in the goods

---

1 There is an obligation to insure the church and its contents so long as funds are available to pay the premium. Where historic buildings or objects are of high value it is sometimes possible, with the specific agreement of the insurerers, to limit cover to the cost of obtaining a good modern replacement. The general duty of repair now extends to the chancel when the incumbent is rector, by virtue of section 52 of the Ecclesiastical Dilapidations Measure 1923. A *lay* rector remains personally liable for the repair of the chancel, except in those cases (probably the majority) where the liability has been voluntarily compounded under the provisions of the Act of 1923, or has been extinguished under the terms of the Tithe Act 1936.

2 A churchyard may be 'closed', i.e. discontinued for burials, by an Order in Council made under the Burial Acts. Under section 18 of the Burial Act 1855, a procedure was established for transferring the duty of maintaining a churchyard so closed in decent order, and its walls and fences repaired, from the churchwardens (or latterly the parochial church council) to the local authority. Except in the City of London where it still applies, this procedure is now superseded by the Local Government Act 1972, section 215. Under the last-mentioned section, if a churchyard has been closed by Order in Council, the parochial church council may serve a written request on the appropriate local authority to take over its maintenance, and the liability for maintenance passes from the parochial church council to the local authority three months after such service. In the case of a churchyard within a civil parish, the notice should be served on the parish council or, if there is no parish council, on the chairman of the parish meeting; and in any other case, it should be served on the district council or London borough council in whose area the churchyard is situated. But when the notice is served on a parish council or the chairman of a parish meeting, the parish council or meeting may, by passing an appropriate resolution and by giving written notice thereof both to the parochial church council and to the district council before the expiration of the three months' period, transfer its liability to the district council. In order to avoid inconvenience to local authorities, however, parochial church councils are urged to give informal notice twelve months before they wish the local authority to assume responsibility; but it would be wise to follow this in due course with the formal three months' notice.

3 Property in this context means 'legal ownership'.

and ornaments of the church or their powers duties and liabilities with respect to visitations.[1]

(iii) The like powers duties and liabilities as, immediately before the relevant date, were possessed by the church trustees[2] (if any) for the parish appointed under the Compulsory Church Rate Abolition Act 1868.

(2) All enactments in any Act whether general or local or personal[3] relating to any powers duties or liabilities transferred to the council from the vestry churchwardens or church trustees as the case may be shall subject to the provisions of this Measure and so far as circumstances admit be construed as if any reference therein to the vestry or the churchwardens or church trustees referred to the council to which such powers duties or liabilities have been transferred and the said enactments shall be construed with such modifications as may be necessary for carrying this Measure into effect.

(3) Where any property is applicable to purposes connected with any such powers duties or liabilities as aforesaid, any deed or instrument which could be or could have been made or executed in relation to such property by a vestry,

---

1 Churchwardens thus retain their powers of making 'presentments', and their duties in respect of answering the questions contained in the visitation articles and of attending visitations for the purpose of being admitted to office.

2 'Church trustees' originated from section 9 of the Compulsory Church Rates Abolition Act 1868, which gave power to appoint a body of trustees in any parish for the purpose of accepting, by bequest or otherwise, and of holding, any contributions which might be given to them for ecclesiastical purposes in the parish. Their powers included the investment of funds in their hands, accumulation of the income, and (subject to any conditions attached by the donors) power to pay over such funds to the churchwardens for expenditure on the ecclesiastical purposes of the parish.

The result of this present provision is that all the powers and functions of church trustees have passed to the parochial church council, and the church trustees and the power to appoint them have been swept away. Presumably, in the light of the fact that all the functions of the churchwardens in relation to the financial affairs of the Church have, under section 4(1)(ii)(a), been transferred to the parochial church council, the council should itself apply any funds required for the ecclesiastical purposes of the parish, instead of paying them over to the churchwardens as section 9 of the Act of 1868 originally required.

3 An Act affecting the whole or a considerable part of the realm is said to be a general Act, because it is of general application. A local Act is one which applies to a particular locality, and a personal (sometimes called 'private') Act is one which affects only a particular person or class of persons.

or by churchwardens or church trustees, may be made or executed by the council of the parish concerned.

(4) This Measure shall not affect any enactment in any private or local Act of Parliament under the authority of which church rates[1] may be made or levied in lieu of or in consideration of the extinguishment or of the appropriation to any other purpose of any tithes customary payments or other property or charge upon property which tithes payments property or charge previously to the passing of such Act had been appropriated by law to ecclesiastical purposes or in consideration of the abolition of tithes in any place or upon any contract made or for good or valuable consideration given and every such enactment shall continue in force in the same manner as if this Measure had not been passed.

For the purposes of this subsection 'ecclesiastical purposes' shall mean the building rebuilding enlargement and repair of any church or chapel and any purpose to which by common[2] or ecclesiastical law a church rate is applicable or any of such purposes.

Holding of property for ecclesiastical purposes: educational schemes
5. (1) Subject to the provisions of this Measure, the council of every parish shall have power to acquire (whether by way of gift or otherwise) any property real or personal[3] –
(a) For any ecclesiastical purpose affecting the parish or any part thereof;
(b) For any purpose in connection with schemes (hereinafter called 'educational schemes') for providing

---

1 The reference here is to those church rates, imposed by private or local Acts, which were excepted from abolition by the Compulsory Church Rates Abolition Act 1868; see section 4(1)(i) and the notes thereto. Since the Measure does not affect the enactments imposing such rates, they are still to be levied by the authority originally empowered to do so, and not by the parochial church council.

2 The common law is that part of the law of England, other than statute, which has existed continually since before legal memory. 'Ecclesiastical law' is a vague phrase, but it would certainly include the canon law which, so far as it binds the laity, has long ago become incorporated in the common law or in Acts of Parliament.

3 All property is in law divided into real and personal property. The distinction is technical, but it may be taken that the two classes together embrace every kind of property.

facilities for the spiritual moral and physical training of persons residing in or near the parish.

(2) Subject to the provisions of this Measure and of the general law and to the provisions of any trusts affecting any such property, the council shall have power to manage, administer and dispose of any property acquired under this section.

(3) A council shall have power, in connection with any educational scheme, to constitute or participate in the constitution of a body of managers or trustees or a managing committee consisting either wholly or partly of persons appointed by the council, and may confer on any such body or committee such functions in regard to the implementation of the scheme, and such functions relating to property held for the purposes of the scheme, as the council thinks expedient.

(4) The powers of a council with respect to educational schemes shall be exercised subject to and in accordance with the terms of any undertaking which may have been given by the council to the Secretary of State for Education and Science, Secretary of State for Wales or to any local authority in connection with any financial or other assistance given by the Secretary of State or the authority in relation to the scheme.

(5) A council shall not exercise any of its powers in relation to educational schemes without the consent of the diocesan board of education for the diocese, and any such consent may be given upon such terms and conditions as the committee considers appropriate in all the circumstances of the case.

Supplementary provisions relating to certain property

6. (1) After the commencement of this Measure,[1] a council shall not acquire any interest in land (other than a short lease as hereinafter defined) or in any personal property to be held on permanent trusts, without the consent of the diocesan authority.[2]

(2) Where, at or after the commencement of this Measure, a council holds or acquires an interest in land (other than a

---

1   i.e. 2nd January 1957: see section 10(2). A council may acquire a right of patronage; see p. 50.
2   See section 1.

short lease as hereinafter defined) or any interest in personal property to be held on permanent trusts, such interest shall be vested in the diocesan authority subject to all trusts, debts and liabilities affecting the same, and all persons concerned shall make or concur in making such transfers (if any) as are requisite for giving effect to the provisions of this subsection.

(3) Where any property is vested in the diocesan authority pursuant to subsection (2) of this section, the council shall not sell, lease, let, exchange, charge or take any legal proceedings with respect to the property without the consent of the authority; but save as aforesaid, nothing in this section shall affect the powers of the council in relation to the management, administration or disposition of any such property.

(3A) Where any property which is occupied by a member of the team in a team ministry is vested in the diocesan authority pursuant to subsection (2) of this section and the council proposes to alter or dispose of the property or any part thereof, the council shall –

(a) keep that member informed of matters arising from the proposal;

(b) afford that member an opportunity to express views thereon before taking any action to implement the proposal; and

(c) have regard to those views before taking any such action.

(4) Where any property is vested in the diocesan authority pursuant to subsection (2) of this section, the council shall keep the authority indemnified in respect of:

(a) all liabilities subject to which the property is vested in the authority or which may thereafter be incident to the property;

(b) all rates, taxes, insurance premiums and other outgoings of whatever nature which may from time to time be payable in respect of the property;

(c) all costs, charges and expenses incurred by the authority in relation to the acquisition or insurance of the property or as trustee thereof;

(d) all costs, proceedings, claims and demands in respect of any of the matters hereinbefore mentioned.

(5) The consents required by subsection (3) of this section are additional to any other consents required by law,

either from the Charity Commissioners or the Secretary of State for Education and Science, Secretary of State for Wales or otherwise.

(6) In this section the expression 'short lease' means a lease for a term not exceeding one year, and includes any tenancy from week to week, from month to month, from quarter to quarter, or from year to year.

(7) Any question as to whether personal property is to be held on permanent trusts shall be determined for the purposes of this section by a person appointed by the bishop.

Miscellaneous powers of council

7. The council of every parish shall have the following powers in addition to any powers conferred by the Constitution or otherwise by this Measure –

(i) Power to frame an annual budget of moneys required for the maintenance of the work of the Church in the parish and otherwise and to take such steps as they think necessary for the raising collecting and allocating of such moneys;

(ii) Power to make levy and collect a voluntary church rate for any purpose connected with the affairs of the church including the administrative expenses of the council and the costs of any legal proceedings;[1]

(iii) Power jointly with the minister to appoint and dismiss the parish clerk and sexton or any persons performing or assisting to perform the duties of parish clerk or sexton and to determine their salaries and the conditions of the tenure of their offices or of their employment but subject to the rights of any persons holding the said offices at the appointed day;[2]

(iv) Power jointly with the minister to determine objects to which all moneys to be given or collected in church shall be allocated;

---

1 This is a new power to levy a voluntary church rate, additional to the power to levy such a rate which has been transferred from the vestry to the council; see section 4(1)(i) and the notes thereto. The purposes for which a rate may be levied under the new power would appear to be somewhat wider than those for which a rate may be levied under the transferred power.

2 See Chapter 9. The expression 'appointed day' presumably means 1st July 1921, which is the 'relevant' date as defined in section 1 of the Measure.

(v) Power to make representations to the bishop with regard to any matter affecting the welfare of the church in the parish[1]

Accounts of the council

8. (1) Every council shall furnish to the annual church meeting the audited accounts of the council for the year ending on 31st December immediately preceding the meeting and an audited statement of the funds and property, if any, remaining in the hands of the council at that date.

(2) At least seven days before the annual parochial church meeting, the council shall cause a copy of the said audited accounts and a copy of the said statement to be affixed at or near the principal door of the parish church as required by paragraph (2) of rule 9 of the Church Representation Rules.[2]

(3) The accounts and statement shall be submitted to the meeting for approval, and, if approved, they shall be signed by the chairman of the meeting who shall then deliver them to the council for publication, and the council shall forthwith cause them to be published in the manner provided by the Church Representation Rules.[3]

(4) The accounts of all trusts administered by the council shall be laid before the Diocesan Authority[4] annually.

Powers of bishop

9. (1) The bishop may subject to the provisions of this Measure and the Constitution[5] make rules for carrying this Measure into effect within the diocese.

(2) If any act required by this Measure to be done by any person is not done within such time as the bishop may consider reasonable it may be done by or under the authority of the bishop.

---

1 This places the council in the same position as an individual parishioner who *may* make such representations. In certain circumstances (see p. 85) the church-wardens are under a duty to do so.

2 See p. 107. The relevant rule is now 9(3)(c).

3 Now rule 9(4) of the Church Representation Rules; see p. 107.

4 See section 1.

5 The 'Constitution' means the Constitution of the Church Assembly (now the General Synod) appended to the Church of England Assembly (Powers) Act 1919.

(3) In the event of a council and a minister being unable to agree as to any matter in which their agreement or joint action is required under the provisions of this Measure, such matter shall be dealt with or determined in such manner as the bishop may direct.

(4) During a vacancy in a diocesan see the powers conferred upon the bishop by this section may be exercised by the guardian of the spiritualities.[1]

Short title, commencement, extent and repeals

10. (1) This Measure may be cited as the Parochial Church Councils (Powers) Measure 1956.

(2) This Measure shall come into operation on the second day of January 1957.

(3) This Measure shall extend to the whole of the Provinces of Canterbury and York except the Channel Islands and the Isle of Man:

Provided that, if an Act of Tynwald so provides, this Measure shall extend to the Isle of Man subject to such modifications, if any, as may be specified in such Act of Tynwald. ·

(4) The Parochial Church Councils (Powers) Measure 1921, and the Parochial Church Councils (Powers) (Amendment) Measure 1949, are hereby repealed.

---

1 See p. 1.

12 Conduct of Meetings

The preceding chapters of this book have been designed with a view to placing the rights and duties of the laity in the parishes in their proper and larger context of the Church of which they are members, and to affording guidance to them in the interpretation of their position, especially in the light of modern legislation.

In this concluding chapter some attempt is made to assist them in the normal conduct of their business, particularly in parochial church councils.

The chairman of the council is normally the incumbent of the parish, but in his absence or on his invitation his place is taken by a lay vice-chairman elected by the council. The incumbent is a member of all committees of the council, but not necessarily the chairman of a committee.

The incumbent is primarily responsible for convening parochial church meetings and the parochial church council. In particular, he or she is under a legal duty to convene the annual parochial church meeting not later than 30th April in every year, and at least four meetings of the parochial church council during the year. The provisions of the Church Representation Rules as to the notices of meetings[1] which must be given should be strictly observed; otherwise there is a risk of the proceedings at meetings being invalidated. The incumbent should instruct the secretary as to the form of agenda which is to be sent to the members.

Before the meeting of a parochial church council, the chairman should already have perused the draft minutes of the last meeting, the reading of which should be the first item of the agenda after prayers have been said. They should be compiled by the secretary from notes taken at the time, and should, before the meeting, have been submitted for comment to the incumbent. In their final draft form they should be written in the minute book. It is important to

---

1   See pp. 105, 146.

remember that the minutes are intended to be a record of business transacted. It is unnecessary and sometimes inconvenient to give a detailed account of a discussion. The minutes should state, for example, that Mrs A. proposed, and Mr B. seconded, a resolution (which should be set out in full). If an amendment is proposed and seconded, it should be similarly recorded. The minutes may state the name of any person who spoke in a debate, but this is not necessary. But it should be recorded, e.g., that a resolution or an amendment was carried (or defeated) and the number of votes given on either side in a division should always be stated. It is expressly provided by the rules that if one-fifth of the members of a parochial church council present and voting on a resolution so require, the minutes should record the names of those voting for and against the resolution; also that any member is entitled to require the manner in which his vote was cast to be recorded.[1]

The names of those present at a meeting should always be recorded.

When the minutes have been read, the chairman should ask if they are a correct record. This is not an invitation to discuss the merits of what is recorded but merely to obtain agreement that the record is correct. If exception is taken as to the accuracy of the record, that question may be debated and the council may vote either to accept the record or to amend it.

The chairman should then ask the council for authority to sign the minutes as read, or as amended, and when he has done so, they become the authentic account of the transactions recorded therein, and are receivable in evidence in any court of justice, if produced to that court by the chairman or secretary.

At this stage it is customary to deal with any business arising out of the minutes, other than business which forms a separate item on the agenda. After this has been disposed of, any correspondence received by the secretary (including apologies for non-attendance) should be read and the instructions of the council taken thereon.

Then the other items on the agenda are taken, one by one, and the decision of the council upon each of them arrived at. Voting is by a show of hands, and a resolution is decided by a simple majority of those present and voting, the chairman having a second or casting vote.

It is customary to include at the end of an agenda paper an item

---

1 See p. 148.

called 'Other Business'. It is within the competence of the council to deal with a matter not specifically mentioned on the agenda paper but the Rules require that three-quarters of the members present at the meeting must consent; and even if such consent is forthcoming, the chairman might reasonably, when the matter is important, rule that it is to be adjourned to a future meeting.

It is open to any member, at any stage in the proceedings, to raise a point of order. In doing so he must confine his remarks to the point of order; he should not be allowed to discuss the merits of the matter under debate. Thus it is in order to submit to the chairman that the matter is not one which it is within the competence of the meeting to discuss, but it is not in order to raise *in this way* the question of the expediency of such a discussion.

The decision whether the question is or is not a point of order rests with the chairman and he must decide it. When he has given his decision it must be accepted by the meeting.

Any member may address the council, but unless he is given leave he should not normally speak more than once in relation to the particular matter under discussion. But he should always be allowed to make an explanation or correction of what he has previously said, should he feel that this is desirable in the light of what is said by a member speaking subsequently to him. The chairman may not properly refuse to hear a member, but he has the right to decide on the order in which members may speak, and he may in a proper case stop any member who in his opinion is speaking irrelevantly to the matter under discussion.

If a point of order is raised, the chairman must first make up his mind that it really is a point of order. If he considers that it is, he must decide the point of order at once, i.e. before the general discussion is resumed.

ORGANIZATION OF THE MEETING OF PARISHIONERS AND ANNUAL PAROCHIAL CHURCH MEETING

Since the meeting of parishioners for the purpose of selecting churchwardens is almost invariably held on the same occasion as the annual meeting required by rule 6 of the Church Representation Rules, the procedures associated with both meetings are summarized in the table on page 176.

Step	Reference	Time
(i) Preparation of new electoral roll	Rule 2(4)	Every sixth year after 2007
a) Notice (Appendix 1:3) displayed	Rule 2(4)	For period of fourteen days beginning at least two months before meeting
b) Oral notification at church services	Rule 2(4)	Two Sundays within above fourteen-day period
c) New roll prepared	Rule 2(6)	Not less than fifteen days or more than 28 days before meeting
d) New roll displayed	Rule 2(7)	For continuous period of fourteen days before meeting
(ii) Revision of roll	Rule 2(1)	Years in which new roll not prepared
a) Notice (Appendix 1:2) displayed	Rule 2(1)	Fourteen days before commencement of revision
b) Revision completed	Rule 2(1)	Not less than fifteen or more than 28 days before meeting
c) Revised roll published	Rule 2(3)	For continuous period of fourteen days before meeting
(iii) Notice of convening of annual parochial church meeting displayed	Rule 7(1)	Period including two Sundays before meeting
(iv) Notice of convening of meeting to elect churchwardens	Churchwardens Measure, Section 4(4)	Period including two Sundays before meeting
(v) Nomination for office other than churchwarden	Rule 11(2)	In writing before the meeting; orally or in writing at the meeting
(vi) Written nomination for office of churchwarden (signed by candidate)	Churchwardens Measure, Section 3(3)	Before the meeting
(vii) Meetings	Rule 6(1) Churchwardens Measure, Section 3(1)	Before 30th April
(viii) Admission of churchwardens	Churchwardens Measure, Section 5(1)	Before 31st July

Index